Living in
ISTANBUL

Photography by Jérôme Darblay

Stylist, Caroline Champenois

Preface by Kenizé Mourad
Texts by Lale Apa, Teresa Battesti,
Caroline Champenois, John Freely,
Nedim Gürsel, Tim Hindle,
Arzu Karamani, Gérard-Georges Lemaire

Flammarion
Paris - New York

For Thaïs and Elif, born with this book

Translated from the French by Bernard Wooding
"Visitor's Guide" translated by Bambi Ballard
Copyediting: David Rowe
Design: Marc Walter
Typesetting: Octavio Editions
Editorial Direction: Ghislaine Bavoillot
Color Separation: Colourscan, Paris

Distributed in North America by Rizzoli International Publications, Inc.

Originally published in French as *L'Art de vivre à Istanbul*
© Flammarion, 1993
English-language edition
© Flammarion, 1994

26, rue Racine
Arnaud Panhard et Levassor
75647 Paris Cedex 13

editions.flammarion.com

10 11 12 6 5 4
ISBN: 978-2-0801-3563-6
Dépôt légal: 04/1994

Printed in Italy by Canale, Turin

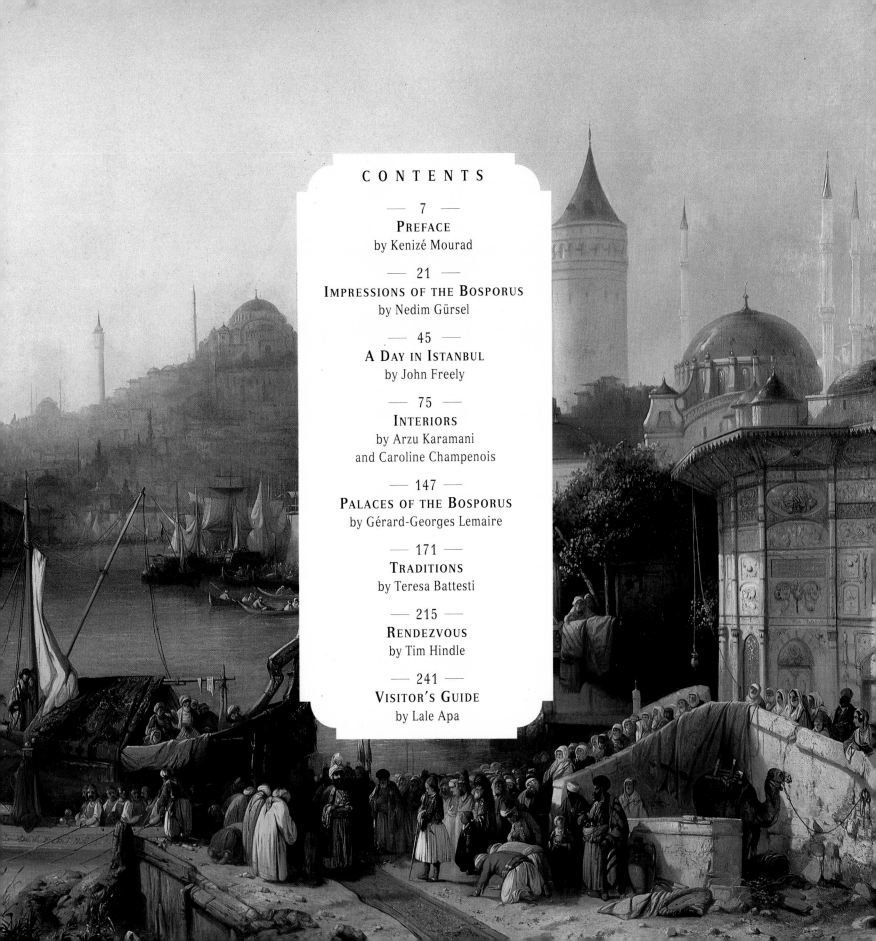

CONTENTS

PREFACE

by Kenizé Mourad

Whenever friends tell me they are planning to visit Istanbul I somehow feel called upon to issue words of warning, like a solicitous daughter who is protective about her mother's beauty and cannot bear others to see that she has fallen on hard times. What I forget is that for people who never knew her when she was in her prime she is still powerfully attractive. And when my friends return and say how much they enjoyed the city, I find myself feeling moved, almost grateful.

It is true, Istanbul is still beautiful, despite the brutalities that she has endured, year after year, at the hands of property developers and speculators. Some 30 years ago, thousands of peasants poured into Istanbul from Anatolia, and it is almost as if this harsh but vibrant region were taking its revenge for the way in which it had been looked down upon by this imperial city, where everything, from the grandest palace to the smallest *yalı*, exudes an air of poetry and refinement.

Unfortunately, in the name of the great god Money, *yalıs* and *konaks* have been destroyed to make way for 'luxury flats' in buildings which look like inner-city tower blocks. Similarly, in the name of the omnipotent Motor Car, the authorities have devastated the west bank of the Bosporus, with its fish restaurants and waterside cafés, in order to build an expressway. And in rather a belated effort in the name of hygiene, the banks of the Golden Horn have been stripped of their historic Byzantine and Ottoman buildings which once housed the craftsmen's workshops. These have been replaced by threadbare lawns, decorated with ugly lamp-posts and red benches bearing the name of one of the city's big banks.

And yet, despite all of this, Istanbul is still a sublime city! Indeed, perhaps this impression of a city wounded and endangered gives Istanbul a nostalgic charm which it never had before. Perhaps for poets and those who see things with the heart, this ephemeral fragility is more moving than the majesty of its past glories. You should hurry to enjoy the pleasures of this all-embracing, sensual city. Hurry to savour 'this city that is like an old *prima donna*,

The Çirağan Palace, where Sultan Murat V, having been deposed in favour of his brother in 1876, lived as a prisoner until his death in 1904. In 1910 the palace, situated on the European shore of the Bosporus near the pretty village of Ortaköy, was gutted by fire and has only recently been restored (opposite page). In the mosque at Ortaköy, the glass droplets of the chandeliers sparkle in the sunlight (below). In the evening there is no spot more enchanting than the gardens of the Çirağan Palace, where the sea stretches before you in an iridescent shimmering of pink and gold. Here you can watch the ships glide slowly by on their journey between the Black Sea and the Golden Horn (overleaf).

covered in jewels and glory', as Cocteau described her, before she becomes a museum in which the only surviving exhibits will be the mosques and palaces, preserved as obligatory stop-off points on the tourist itinerary.

But perhaps I am being unfair, like those elderly residents of Istanbul who turn their backs on the onslaught of vulgarity by shutting themselves away in their old residences

The Dolmabahçe Palace, made entirely of white marble, stretches lazily along the Bosporus. Styles of every country and every era have been mixed together in an opulent disorder.

The exuberance, profusion and whimsical elegance of its decor is somehow endearing, like a child who has dressed up in odds and ends of finery from her mother's wardrobe in an effort to look beautiful. The glittering droplets of chandeliers and candelabras form a cascade of gold and crystal (above and opposite page).

and retreating into their memories. Perhaps Istanbul has lost something of its nobility, but it has gained much in the sunlit whirl of its everyday life, with its smells and its colours. New blood now courses through the veins of this haughty, blasé city, supplied by the peasants from Anatolia, who have brought with them their traditions, their appetites, their down-to-earth realism and simple beliefs.

The peasants live in *gecekondu*, makeshift houses which are put up overnight. They are illegal, but tolerated by a government which has no other way of housing these economic refugees. Over the years, the *gecekondu* on the outskirts of Istanbul have multiplied to the

point where they now house more than half the city's population. They are not slums, as one might suppose. Rather, they are places where the country has been transplanted to the city. The women wear headscarves, baggy trousers and smocks, groups of men squat in the streets chatting, and the sheep are left to wander freely in the dirt roads.

Here, as in the traditional quarters of old Istanbul, hospitality is very important. There is no question of refusing a *çay*, the tea that is offered as a gesture of friendship. Foreigners are welcome, as long as they ask permission before taking photographs; the Turks have a powerful sense of their own dignity, they are discreet and expect the same of their guests. If you respect the basic rules of etiquette, you will be warmly welcomed, because, as the Koran says, 'the stranger is the envoy of God'. If you are invited to share a modest meal of onions, white cheese and bread, do not refuse because you will give offence.

This hospitality and the qualities of patience and wisdom which one reads in the eyes of these newcomers are a lesson in humanity which the city is now learning from the countryside. It is something which should give heart to those Istanbulites who complain about the 'barbaric invasion' of their city and the resulting deterioration.

As for myself, if my grandmother's *yalı*—the 'lace palace'—has been turned into the Ortaköy bathing club and the sultana's drawing room has now become a volleyball court, where I hold my breath every time the ball comes within inches of the delicate painted decorations on the ceiling, I tell myself that it really doesn't matter. At least the *yalı* is still

Istanbul's verdant cemeteries are sanctuaries of peace. Sometimes, as at Üsküdar on the Asian shore (above right) and at Eyüp (above and below right) on the Golden Horn, they extend right to the hilltops. Each tombstone is a work of art. Some are sculpted with ceremonial turbans, the size of which generally indicates the social status of the deceased.

standing. It lives a new life, torn between amusement and disapproval at the sight of the men and women in their swimming trunks and bikinis who have replaced the princesses in long silk dresses.

Next door, the *yalı* of the elegant 'butterfly sultana' has been turned into a school, filled with the happy sounds of shouting children. Its gilt and frescoes are peeling, its walls are covered in graffiti and you have the feeling that it might collapse at any moment under the thundering feet of the children as they stampede up and down the corridors and staircases. But I sense that it is proud and happy at being able to house this bursting energy of youth and hope. At any event, these two *yalıs* are more fortunate than the *yalı* of Sultana Fatimeh, the youngest of the three sisters, which suffered the indignity of being demol-

ished in order to make way for the first bridge over the Bosporus.

I often used to walk by the charred remains of the Çirağan Palace, trying to imagine what

'An eastern cemetery is one of the finer things of the Orient. No wall, no ditch, no fence, no separation whatsoever. They can be found scattered haphazardly across town and country alike, like death itself, next to life and appearing without warning.' So wrote Flaubert in 1850. At the Pierre Loti café in Eyüp, which one reaches at the end of a long walk through the graveyard (above left and below), one can watch and dream as the sun sets on the iridescent waters of the Golden Horn.

life must have been like for my family, imprisoned there for 30 years. The ruins have now been restored and are enjoying a new life as a hotel. The exterior has been painstakingly reconstructed, but the interior, sadly, has been painted in garish colours instead of the traditional delicate pastels of the Ottoman palaces and fitted with a huge escalator flanked by fluorescent lights.

I watched as Istanbul's interior designers and architects attempted to prevent this particular piece of vandalism. I even became involved myself. But what could we do against the power of foreign investors? I remain hopeful that people will eventually realize that beauty can be as profitable as vulgarity and that one day the soul will be restored to this palace, once considered the finest in Istanbul. Perhaps then the ghosts of the three sultanas and of their father,

the romantic Sultan Murat V, will return to visit these salons, once lit by the gentle light of crystal chandeliers, and once again the rustle of silk trains will be heard on the marble staircases.

Fortunately the Çirağan is the only palace to have 'benefited' from such 'modernization'. The other major palaces—Topkapı, Dolmabahçe, Yıldız and Beylerbeyi—have either been carefully preserved or restored to their former splendour. The most delightful palaces, however, tend to be the smaller ones which the tourists do not visit. There is Göksu, on the Sweet Waters of Asia, where caïques carpeted with gold-embroidered velvet used to glide past, and Ilhamur, which today finds itself in the heart of Istanbul, albeit protected by its park. One can wander around them unhindered by crowds and perhaps pick a rose—just one from each bush, as Sultan Reçat

At Topkapı Palace, in the gallery of the 36 sultans who, over the course of six centuries, made and unmade the empire, I have often stopped in front of the portrait of Mehmet II, the Conqueror. In his hand he holds a rose and the contrast between the gentleness of this gesture and the icy coldness of his gaze is striking. It was in 1453, during the reign of this sultan who put an end to the

Byzantine Empire, that Constantinople became Istanbul (above). Far from the bustle of the city and the crowds of tourists, the small palace of Ilhamur is a charming and little-known retreat. An exuberant marble rococo building, it was once the sultans' hunting lodge. Today, because of the constant expansion of Istanbul, it is in the heart of the city (opposite page). On the Asian shore, at Küçüksu, the little palace of Göksu is a delicate jewel on the Sweet Waters of Asia (right). Formerly a residence for heads of state on official visits, it is now open to the public.

recommended to his wives, because, as he said, one should not spoil nature's work.

A love of nature is deeply rooted in the soul of the Turkish people, who have been described as violent. This may be true if their honour is affronted, but Turks are above all poetic and sensitive, sometimes to the point of sentimentality. One of their favourite activities is to go and watch the sun setting on the Bosporus, when the rush hour is over and you can hear the birds singing again. Entire families sit and watch, sometimes with tears in their eyes, as the horizon becomes a blaze of gold and purple, silhouetting the slender shapes of minarets and the domes of palaces. Another favourite outing is the 'moon party'. People hire a boat or take the ferry out to the Princes' Isles, and spend the whole night between sky and water, drinking *raki* and eating *mezes*.

Istanbulites also like to visit the big cemeteries, havens of greenery where the graves are marked by white marble columns, decorated with carved turbans or fezzes for the men and graceful cornucopias for the women. The gravestones made from semi-precious stones and decorated with miniature fezzes or garlands of roses mark the graves of children. In the old days families would come and spend the whole day here, picnicking in the company of their deceased relations.

One of the most attractive cemeteries is in Eyüp, overlooking the Golden Horn. It was here that Pierre Loti came to dream of Aziyadé, and the little café which bears his name, furnished with sofas and flanked by a terrace which is fragrant with wisteria, is a delightful place in which to immerse oneself in the past—

always assuming that you are not put off by the Coca-Cola sign hanging over the entrance. But it is like that everywhere in Istanbul. You have to have a filtering eye capable of shutting out the intrusions of modern life if you want to enjoy the city's innumerable pleasures.

The streets of Istanbul provide a constant spectacle: the bread seller with his *simit*—small rounds of bread spiced with sesame, which he carries in a pyramid on his head with the casualness of a tightrope walker; the nut sellers, with their almonds artistically arranged on a bed of fresh green leaves; the sellers of multicoloured *limonata*, with their big glass bottles of cordial; and the bands of shoeshine boys, equipped with magnificent planished-copper brush boxes, who tussle over the shoes of tourists.

The presence of this child labour reminds us, as if we needed reminding, that despite its modern buildings and its Europeanized elites, Istanbul is still the Orient. It is an Orient which reveals itself at every step: in the open-air cafés where the exclusively male clientele

spends its time absorbed in interminable games of backgammon; in the shady courtyards of ancient caravanserais, where the hookah smokers seem to be savouring eternity; and in the street cries of the confectioners selling their *loukhoums*, 'as tender as a maiden's breast', and those of the water seller, harnessed in his superb leather water-carrier with its array of glasses. The water sellers generally do good business in the bazaar and the older quarters where piped water is not always available. People are demanding with regard to their water and an Istanbulite with a refined palate can often tell you from which spring the water comes.

There are fountains everywhere in Istanbul. In the Ottoman period, building a fountain was regarded as an act of charity by the philanthropic rich. It was a way of helping the poor and at the same time a chance to vaunt their wealth. Many are now disused, but some still provide places where women can meet to gossip and trade secrets.

To penetrate even more deeply into the private world of these women you have to visit a *hamam*, such as the one at Ortaköy. There, in the steam rooms, with the light filtering through small panels of stained glass in the cupolas, the women stretch out and relax, refreshing themselves occasionally with water from the marble basins. In the centre a half-naked masseuse busies herself, rubbing with her horsehair glove until your skin turns lobster-red. Then she massages you energetically with an oil used formerly in harems and reputed to have aphrodisiac powers.

But remember, a visit to the *hamam* cannot be carried out in a couple of hours. It is a day-long affair. People bring refreshments and exchange cakes with evocative names, such as *dilber dudaklar* (my beloved's lips), *hanım göbeği* (lady's navel) and *vezir parmağı* (vizier's finger). Sometimes, carried away be her state of sensual well-being, a woman will get up and begin swaying her hips and arms, while others accompany her with rhythmic songs and a clicking of fingers. In an instant one finds one-

self transported a century or two back in time, into the heated and disturbing complicity of the harems of Ottoman times.

At any moment—at a street corner, in one of the sultans' exquisite tea pavilions, or perhaps in an artisan's shop—the delights of the past are liable to spring out at you. Istanbul, a city between two continents, is also a city between two epochs, and if you have an open heart and an open mind you will undoubtedly enjoy the trip.

But to really appreciate Istanbul you will have to learn *rehavet*—to breathe time, to savour it in small mouthfuls, slowly . . . like a gourmet.

Circumcision is still an occasion for big celebrations. Boys, dressed like princes in red velvet and white satin, consecrate their new status as men with a pilgrimage to the mosque at Eyüp. There they seek out the tomb of the Prophet's standard-bearer, Eyüp El Ansari, who fell at the siege of Constantinople in the seventh century and has since become an inspiring example of courage.

The ceremony takes place in the family home, where the 'circumcision bed' is richly decorated for the occasion. This one is exhibited in the Sadberk Hanim Museum (opposite page).
The 'lace palace', an old carved wooden building overlooking the Bosporus (above), now serves as the Ortaköy bathing club. Selma and her family left the *yalı* in 1923, when Mustafa Kemal passed a law exiling all the princes and princesses of the Ottoman family. The law was repealed for the princesses in 1952 and for the princes only at the end of the 1970s.

The *hamam*, unrivalled for relaxing the mind and the body, is a popular meeting place in Istanbul. Sometimes a Turkish woman will hire an entire *hamam* to entertain her friends. The tradition of holding receptions at the *hamam* for events such as marriages is still alive and provides an unforgettable experience for those present. The *hamam* at Cağaloğlu (above), in Stamboul, dates from the eighteenth century. The marble *hararet*, or steam-room (right), is particularly splendid.

IMPRESSIONS OF THE BOSPORUS

by Nedim Gürsel

From a room in a corbelled wooden house lapped
by the waters of the Bosporus, a writer
describes the changing light of the strait, the lush
green of its hills, the never-ending ballet of the
passing ships, and the various ports of call on a ferry
trip from one shore to the other, before plunging
into the bustle of the crowds in the
heart of the old city.

One of the six minarets of the Blue Mosque, with its *serefe* (balcony), towers above the gold crescent which crowns the central dome. 'My country of leaden domes and factory chimneys is the work of my people,' said Nâzim Hikmet, the great Turkish poet who died in exile (preceding double page). At Kanlıca, the Ethem Pertev *yalı* is notable for the elegance and refinement of its architecture and the lacelike quality of its woodwork. Below it are two boathouses, which, although empty today, once housed large ceremonial caïques with sides decorated in gold-leaf (below). Further along, on one of the café terraces, one can sample the famous sugared yoghurts of Kanlıca (sweet yoghurt is rare in Turkey) while savouring the delights of the Bosporus. On the Asian shore, the waters of the Bosporus are silvery at dawn, becoming dark blue in the course of the morning, and then changing to indigo. As dusk approaches they turn mauve. Fishermen's boats bob on the waters night and day, in the company of cormorants (right).

For many years I used to wake up early. At the time I was staying on the Asian shore of the Bosporus, in this city that I love so much, this city which has followed me everywhere and which, like a red-hot iron, is branded on my memory. Every morning I would get up at the hour of morning prayers to write. But if I had known that one day I would end up dropping everything and hiding away in a room in this old *yalı*, and that I would be carried along with the autumn days in which the morning mists were dispersed early by the swirling breezes which crossed the Bosporus under my corbelled window, I would have given up writing this story—a story which, as yet, was hardly more perceptible than the movements of the underwater currents of the Bosporus itself. We had rented a *yalı* for the holidays, and I would have left it at the same time as my friends; like them, I would have been back at work in Paris by the first week in September. We'd had a good summer. Far from the noise of the city and the August heat that made life unbearable in blocks of flats in the centre of the city and the shaded cafés by the sea. We were good friends. We always got on well, whether we were on the fresh waters of the Bosporus, on the seaweedy granite blocks of the jetty in front of the *yalı*, or out in the evening, savouring the smell of grilled fish from some nearby restaurant. In the mornings we would breakfast in the garden. Then we would go for a swim, or take a boat trip together, and when we withdrew to our rooms, it was always with an impatience to meet again a short while later, to chat over a glass of tea. This is how August was spent, in an atmosphere of peace and calm, and finally our holiday came to an end. On the last day, as everyone else was preparing to leave, I told my friends that I intended to stay on in Istanbul for a bit longer, in order to work on a set of archives in the Topkapı museum. I would return a short while later, to resume my course at the university. They all agreed.

Being alone, I told the owner that I would take my meals in the kitchen, that I would no longer use the main dining room, and that, if he so wished, he could draw the curtains, cover the armchairs and tables, put the divan cushions back in the cupboard, and shut up all the rooms, except for the one with the corbelled window overlooking the sea. In the whole of this huge *yalı* there was nobody left but me. At last I was going to be able to embark on writing the story that I had been planning for the whole summer, and which I had been constantly postponing, a task that, in a way, I did not succeed in accomplishing because I was endlessly thinking about it, lying in the sun on the quayside. Although I had collected all kinds of books and documents on my theme, I needed a word to start from. Each morning I watched the mists dispersing in front of me, and the opposite shore seemed so close that I could have touched it. I watched, enraptured, as the ramparts shone in the first light of day, with their white walls guarding the Devil's Current (one of the many currents of the Bosporus) at the narrowest point of the strait. As I watched this splendid fortress—which is now hemmed in by concrete blocks—I thought about the period when it was built, and of the Empire in its days of glory. And there it was, directly opposite me. Clinging to its hillside on the other shore, it was as close as the water, as clear as the day. But, obeying a bad habit I have, I needed to begin with a word.

When one sees the Bosporus Bridge
suspended above baroque minarets,
should one speak of contrast or
harmony? The Ortaköy Mosque
is surrounded by huge quays.
During the reign of Abdül Mecit I
in the nineteenth century, these
were the setting for the ceremony of
the sovereign's arrival for Friday
prayers (above).
'And soon begins the frantic invasion
of boatmen, customs officers and
porters; a hundred caïques assail us,
and all these people, who come
flooding aboard, speak and shout in all
the languages of the Levant,' wrote
Pierre Loti about disembarking at the
port of Istanbul. Nowadays, cruise
liners are moored side by side
in the port where silently they wait
for the moment of departure (right).

The fortress at Rumeli Hisar was built in 1425 by Mehmet the Conqueror just before the siege of Constantinople, in order to control the passage of ships through the strait, and to prevent Byzantium from receiving assistance via the Black Sea. With its outer walls flanked with towers, it still dominates the narrowest stretch of the Bosporus, from where the waters then flow down past Saray Point. The quay and the road which nowadays run along the shore are more recent additions: in earlier times parts of the eastfacing walls of Rumeli Hisar were bathed by the waters of the Bosporus.

Sultan Mehmet II—at that time he was not yet known as the Conqueror—was not, of course, to know that centuries after him a writer was going to adopt the name of *Boğazkesen* (Throat-cutter, the name given to Mehmet II's fortress and a pun on the Turkish words for 'Bosporus' and 'throat', which are almost homonyms) as the title of a forthcoming story, any more than he could have known that future historians would one day be researching the throatcutters and the throats that had been cut that darkened his reign, and that the people he had impaled or sawn in half would return to haunt his dreams and demand that he account for the blood that had been

spilt. Anyway, when Sultan Mehmet, by now indeed the Conqueror, with the fine sensual mouth and the black beard that we know from Bellini's portrait, returned to Üsküdar in the imperial caïque, did he know that the rose that he held in the painted miniature, between those sensuous, gout-inflamed fingers, this three-petalled imperial rose picked in the palace gardens, would one day wither and die? Of course he didn't. As the soldiers of Rumeli crossed to Anatolia to set off on campaigns, Sultan Mehmet the Conqueror, son of Sultan Murat Khan the Victorious, 49 years old, posted in the shade of the aigrettes which fluttered in the port of Üsküdar, did he remember the fortress which he had built at the age of 20, and the enthusiasm of the nights of pleasure of his youth? We might suppose so.

At that time, he used to ride up and down the shore on horseback for days on end, studying the lie of the land and observing the currents. Eventually he found the perfect spot. He decided that the fortress was to be built on the side of the hill, on the site of the ruins of the monastery of the archangel Michael, directly opposite Akçahisar, which had been built by his grandfather Yıldırım Beyazıt. At this point the terrain slopes steeply down towards the water, forming a promontory extending towards the Asian shore, and the narrowing of the strait meant that the currents were faster here.

Perhaps he was not aware of the fact that many years, in fact centuries, earlier, Darius had also passed by this spot on his way to fight the Greeks. However, he would not have forgotten how, when Ladislas, King of Hungary, marched on him just after he had acceded to the throne, his father, Murat Khan the Victorious, faced with Frankish ships barring the Dardanelles, had sailed up the coastline as far as Akçahisar, and there, with the aid of God and the help of Genoese ships, upon payment of one ducat per soldier, had been able to help him by crossing the Bosporus at precisely that point. How could he have forgotten, even though he had been a mere child at the time, sheltering under the wing of the Grand Vizier Halil Paşa in his palace at Andrinople? A child who, for all his youth, was endowed with great intelligence and nurtured dreams of grandeur.

As I finished writing these historical notes, dawn was breaking. I turned out the light and sat at the window with a cigarette. It was still dark outside. You couldn't see the shore opposite. A Russian cargo ship, with all its lights out, passed by, leaving a wake behind it. For a long time I watched the white trail that its propellor left in the water. Then, feeling relaxed at having finished my work for the day, I stretched out on the bed and stared at the ceiling. I wasn't tired. I thought about how that the fortress now served no useful purpose, and about the traffic that had been passing up and down the Bosporus, without interruption, for centuries. Who knows how many ships have passed along these waters—paddle-driven, sail-driven, propellor-driven, each with their crew and their respective complement of passengers! How many of them had reached port safely and how many had returned? A faint light illuminated the ceiling. The interior of the room slowly began to brighten. The light spread until the whole ceiling was covered. Suddenly a swathe of blue invaded the room. I saw the waves of the sea moving on the ceiling. At that same instant the white of the walls disappeared, giving way to a flow of colours. In my mind's eye I could see the rocks of the Bosporus, covered

The *yalıs* of Kuzguncuk were a favourite haunt of the sultans, masters of three continents who came here by caïque for holidays with their entourages. In those days, behind the high garden walls, the sound of lutes, viols and zithers mingled with the voices of minstrels, and only seagulls and the liveried oarsmen disturbed the surrounding waters.

Anadolu Hisar, an Anatolian fortress which Ottoman historians call Güzelce Hisar (The Beautiful Fortress) was built by Beyazıt I in 1431. The waters of the Bosporus are reflected in the Venetian mirrors decorating the salons of *yalıs* built on what were once loading jetties for the fortress which the ferry passes by before arriving at the landing stage (below).

On the Asian shore, ancient and modern *yalıs* sit side by side. Many of them belonged to the Empire's great dignitaries. While many of these summer residences have been restored, others have been abandoned to a wretched fate—for example the residence of Amcazade Hüseyin Paşa near Körfez, which dates from the end of the seventeenth century (opposite page). This old building today stands forlornly, with its worm-eaten walls and its great salon, just above the waterline where the waves threaten to engulf it at any moment. The fishing season begins in autumn, when shoals of bluefish come back down the Bosporus (overleaf).

with green seaweed, the black sheen of mussels, and sleepy crabs. In the depths of the ceiling swam *lapinas* with iridescent scales, silvery fish and ink-black blennies. I dived into the swelling waves.

I was awakened by a noise. My bed was moving violently, as if it was being shaken by an earthquake. The furniture was creaking and the windows juddering. At first I thought that a ship had gone off course and had hit the *yalı*. But as I gathered my wits and sat up on the bed I realised that the noise was coming from downstairs. I got up immediately and hurried down to the floor below. Nothing out of the ordinary there. Whatever it was, the whole *yalı* was still being shaken to its foundations, as if it were being shelled. When I went down to the next floor, the noise became even louder and plaster was beginning to crumble from the walls. The crystal chandelier on the ceiling was swaying slightly and the mirror swinging from side to side on the wall. I still couldn't work out what was happening. Massive blows rained in on the building, as if the *yalı* was

about to be destroyed by some mad giant who had broken free of his chains. Once I had gathered my senses together, I realized that something was happening down in the boathouse, because that seemed to be the eye of the storm. That was definitely where the noise was coming from. With some trepidation I went down to the landing stage. I undid the mooring rope of the caïque and took the oars. As I rowed round to the entrance of the boathouse, I saw that a huge dolphin was thrashing against the walls, sending up showers of spray in its panic. The creature had somehow found its way into the interior of the building and, finding itself trapped, was now struggling to escape. It thrashed about desperately with its tail, splashing water right up to the ceiling. For a moment it seemed to relax; then it turned its head towards the entrance. Finding itself in slightly deeper water, it seemed reassured. I presumed that it had gone in there following a shoal of tuna. Before leaving those dark confines, it seemed to pause to take a look around at the mossy walls, the caïque pontoon, which had not been used for years, and the dilapidated, mouldering beams. The dolphin looked at the elegant turquoise-blue caïques, and at their slender, delicately sculpted wooden hulls. Then it dived and passing right before my eyes, disappeared into the blue of the Bosporus. I went back to my room to return to my slumbers, and I dreamed of the dolphin, now free, roaming the blue waters of the Sea of Marmara, its skin glistening under the sun, as it leapt in the water and played with the foaming waves. I abandoned myself to the sunlit waves reflected on the ceiling, and, before I fell asleep, I decided that my

story would deal with the tragic end of a young man taken prisoner of war.

The fortress glowed in the light of the dawn. The mist had gone. By the light of day, I could pick out the line of round towers on the opposite shore with their linking stone walls, beyond which lay a jumble of houses where modern villas stood in the midst of wooden buildings. Up above, at the top of the hill, trees were silhouetted, as if in a shadow theatre. It's always like this. In the morning light the fortress seems to come so close that you could touch it. In the afternoon, as the sun follows its course down the Bosporus, slowly sinking towards the opposite shore, the light changes again. The colours fade slightly. A strange mist rises from the sea, and after a while the fortress is almost completely hidden from view. I wait impatiently for the morning, when once again it will rise up before me like the genie from Aladdin's magic lamp. As I wait, my eyelids slowly close and I abandon myself to the drowsiness of a siesta.

When I awoke, I found that the light on the ceiling had taken on an orangish tinge. I got up and pulled the curtains aside. The blazing light from the sun as it set behind the ramparts flooded into the room as the hooter sounded on the 7.20 ferry which was pulling in at the landing stage below. I was thrilled at this transformation in time and colour. I didn't want to light the lamp. Not a leaf moving. No ships passing. Not a single cricket chirping in the garden. Everything stood still. There I was, a person without either past or future, a man possessed, a lone soul exiled from himself, abandoned in a *yalı*, in the grip of his own imagination.

I would have wanted her to arrive in an imperial caïque, the gilt woodwork of its hull shining as it had done in the days of the Empire, with a silver eagle at the prow, the chief eunuch gripping the tiller, a caïque which dives into the current with the vivacity of a seagull, jolting the feather cushions in the cabin enclosed by gold-trimmed satin curtains and the dark faces of the standing oarsmen, pulling hard at their oars. At the quayside the caïque would bob in the moonlight as she disembarked. Wearing a *feradje* which would reveal her shapely body, she would place her satin-slippered foot on the quayside, and the wind would lift her delicate muslin veil to reveal two jet-black eyes, looking at me. In my inner soul I would feel the power of that glance, so charged with desire, and I would shiver at the joy of our secret encounter. Another evening she would come knocking at my door, at dinner time.

That morning, everything seemed to have emerged from a deep sleep at just the same time

Büyükdere lies on the European shore just up from the Bay of Tarabya, which was a favourite holiday resort of the Phanariots. Embassies had their summer residences in this charming spot (opposite page).
One of these splendid *yalıs* houses the Sadberk Hanım Museum, which contains a rich collection of antiques and traditional costumes.
At stalls laden with tomatoes,

cucumbers and lemons, one can eat freshly caught fish, which are grilled to perfection on a charcoal grill (below left). Together with the few cafés that are still to be found at the water's edge, the ferry landing stages provide the most welcoming places by the Bosporus. This is where one arranges to meet one's friends to 'go into town' when one lives on the shores of the Bosporus. At Rumeli Kavaği, the last stop on the European shore, one can savour the delights of giant mussels arranged on skewers and cooked in oil (above).

The landing stage at Beşiktaş is built directly in front of the statue of the famous admiral Hayrettin Paşa, known in the West as Barbarossa. One enters via a magnificent waiting room, where the yellow and red doors remind you of the sunny days of summer. Here you can sit on a wooden bench, waiting for your ferry, savouring the cool breeze and the foaming waves of the Bosporus.

as me. Still in the drowsiness of its morning mists, the sea—like the seagulls swooping to and fro before my eyes—was lapping below my corbelled window. I dressed and went down to the jetty. As the day dawned, the waves rolled up the Bosporus. How long had it been since I had last sunk into such a long, deep sleep? Even the shock of the cool waves lapping at my feet and splashing up towards my face did not wake me fully. I was finding it hard to shrug off the heavy night. As during the summer days that I had spent with my friends, I wanted to prepare a strong tea and go and drink it in the garden, next to the fish pond. Then, I don't know why, I told myself that the aura of the old days which

emanated from that garden would probably have disappeared. The lawn was probably yellowing and the leaves of the plane trees would surely have started to fall. As for the fish in the pond, maybe they'd ended up in the next-door neighbour's aquarium. I thought of the isolated bench where we used to sit in the mornings, of the flowers withering for lack of care at the edge of the pond, and of the fountain, the moss-covered stones, and of the garden's little pavilion. Yes, there was even a pavilion up against one wall, where we used to sit in summer—it must still be there. But, for some reason that I couldn't fathom, I wasn't in the mood. I didn't want to go and sit there, to sip my tea and gaze

On the first floor of the Beşiktaş landing stage a tearoom takes over from the itinerant tea sellers (or cold drink sellers) who are continually accosting travellers during the crossing. Here one has the chance to play backgammon or dominoes (left), but watch out you don't miss your ferry!

'My beloved has enrolled in the Navy . . .' So says a popular song. Every Saturday, students on shore leave from the naval college at Heybeli, one of the Princes' Isles, take the boat to Istanbul, where cinemas and discotheques beckon (above). The bustle of the city must come as rather a shock after the peace and quiet of their island.

at withered roses next to a dried up pond. I would have to accept now that the garden was a thing of the past, that its beauty would remain in the memory of days past. Was it the melancholy of that autumn morning, or the heaviness of sleep that was still weighing on me? Or perhaps it was neither? Was it, rather, the vague and subconscious influence of dreams I could not even recall? No matter. I decided to go into town. Maybe that would help me escape the heaviness that was oppressing me and the uncomfortable feeling of having started a day so dismally. This was the first time since I'd begun to write my story that I had felt the need to go out.

I followed the road that led to the ferry pier. For a long while I couldn't see the sea because of the *yalıs*, or rather because of the shapeless concrete buildings interspersed with the few remaining *yalıs*, which hid the shoreline. Cars, taxis and the first buses of the morning travelled by. I thought of boarding one of them and travelling to the end of the line then, wherever I happened to end up, walking wherever the fancy took me, right through until evening, in the hopes of ridding myself of whatever it was that was depressing me. But I decided to take the ferry instead. A trip down to Eminönü on a ferry would do me good. As I passed through the turnstile and stepped onto the landing stage, I felt a great joy at being close to the Bosporus again. I had fallen into bad habits! The dark blue of the Bosporus in the morning, its purplish waters at dusk, the sun sparkling on the water, the emeraldgreen woods on the opposite shore, and the fortress of Rumeli Hisar had become engraved on my memory. They had become part of my being, of my reclusive life in the *yalı*, something which I would never

be able to renounce. The first ferry of the morning appeared, surging out of the mist, and drew close to the landing stage, leaving in its wake small waves which rippled regularly along the shoreline. I went on board, sat down on the semi-circular bench in the stern, and abandoned myself to the gentle movement of the sea. We were being carried by the current in the direction of Kandilli.

The fog thickened. After a while we could no longer see either of the shores. On the left you could just make out the off-white shape of the Küçüksu Palace. It looked more like some abandoned building out of a horror film. The meadow of Göksu had melted into the mist, as had the plane trees, the road, and even the hill of Sevda. Then I heard the call to prayer coming through the mist, and knew that we were approaching the landing stage at Kandilli. Just at that moment, as if by arrangement, all the ferries in the area began to sound their foghorns. The hooting merged with the strident cries of seagulls and the slapping of mooring ropes on the surface of the water,

The Mecidiye Mosque at Ortaköy was one of the places where you could see the sultan during the ceremony after prayers, surrounded by courtiers and oarsmen standing to attention with their oars raised. Here one can also visit a Greek church, an Armenian church and a synagogue. Second-hand book sellers display new and antique books, among which one can sometimes find 'treasures'.

One can also eat (rather well) or sip a tea 'the colour of rabbit's blood' as one watches huge ships passing, with seagulls diving in their wake (opposite page). In the little café at Çengelköy, where this photograph was taken, the card-players rarely look up to admire the scenery. However, it is from here that one has the best view of the Bosporus Bridge and the overcast sky filtering a grey light through onto the hills of the shore opposite (above).

When spring arrives the Judas trees flower among the cypresses along the hills of the Bosporus (right). Istanbul's cemeteries have always held a fascination for writers, including the French writers Gautier, Nerval and Loti. It is true that these graveyards are sometimes something of a wilderness, with the grass and flowers vying with the stone pillars topped with turbans, which, half buried, emerge from the ground. However, the cemeteries on the hills which overlook the Bosporus, particularly those on the European shore, have a different air. They are more ordered, better maintained and relatively more recent (below). The sight of the roofs of the Çirağan Palace, seen from a pavilion in the Yıldız Park (opposite page) shows the proximity of the two palaces that were inhabited by the Ottoman sultans during the nineteenth century. The Çirağan Palace was built for Abdül Aziz two years before he was overthrown by the Young Ottomans who proclaimed the First Constitution in 1876. Abdül Hamit II, his successor, who lived for a long time in the Yıldız Palace, was overthrown by the Young Turks in 1908.

drowning out the call to prayer. After Kandilli, as we headed across to the opposite shore, the fog became even thicker. We could no longer hear a thing. On we went, with the water lapping agreeably round us, neither seeing nor knowing where we were going. It was as if ours was the first ferry to have travelled those waters. We were in the hands of a virgin nature, with no other humans present, the fish and seagulls our only companions. I thought back to thousands of years previously, to when this stretch of sea had been formed, when the waters of the Black Sea, having filled the shallow valley of the Bosporus, had finally met the warmer, salty waters of the Mediterranean. I wondered what it must have been like for the fish at the moment when these two seas had collided together, merging in a violent embrace. There were no humans in those

days, but there were fish, and even sea monsters. The waters filled the valley, thereby lowering the hills, and a current was formed, a current which travelled from north to south on the surface, but moved in the opposite direction in the valley bottom. Since that day, who knows how many shoals of fish, fleets of ships, bodies of unfortunate suicides who had hurled themselves into the deep waters, or even murder victims, had been swept away by this current. Now we were the ones who were being swept away, with our ferry struggling to reach the other shore towards the Sea of Marmara, and the current bearing us down by Leander's Tower. I let myself be carried away by these gloomy thoughts for a while, then realized that my fears were unfounded. The captain, a man of great experience, drove the boat full speed ahead from the Cape of the Current to Bebek

Bay, and used the Devil's Current to get him there. As I struggled with my thoughts, musing on the history of Istanbul and wondering what it must have been like during the prehistoric period, the early morning fog began to lift, and the Bosporus began to show itself in its true light. The turbulent waters, the houses along the shoreline, the outlines of the hills began to appear in the morning light, and the white ships at anchor in Bebek Bay became gradually more distinct.

As the ferry went on its way, I felt less oppressed, less affected by the murkiness of the long night and of the chaotic dreams and visions linked to my *Boğazkesen* story. I felt as if I were being reborn from the ashes, as if this were my first ferry trip down the Bosporus. I was reliving and rediscovering everything— the gentle lapping of the waves, the cool breeze, the strident calls of seagulls, the ships with their foghorns sounding in the mist, and the soft light of the September sun as it melted the mist and gradually brought the opposite shore to life.

At one moment an enormous ocean liner passed close to us. The wash splashed the passengers who were sitting all along the side of our ferry. They didn't so much as shift in their seats. They continued sipping their tea in silence as if nothing had happened. When we approached the Bebek landing stage, I saw the little dome of the mosque at the water's edge, and its minuscule minaret, almost like a toy. In the park, the trees had not yet begun to lose their leaves. The trunk of a huge old plane tree which was beginning to split in two, had been filled with concrete in order to prevent it breaking apart.

We then headed for Arnavutköy, and then on to Ortaköy and Beşiktaş. At each landing stage I felt as if I had completed one more stage of a journey that I was making for the first time. Along the shore, where concrete buildings were intermixed with old *yalıs*, I could see women who had just got up, and men in pyjamas smoking their first cigarette of the day on their balconies. They were

unknown people to me, belonging to a world which I was discovering for the first time—distant, curious and somehow unreal. But the truth was that I was the one who was unreal and outside life. Ever since I had shut myself away in the *yalı*, I had forgotten that there were other people in this world, other places. My story had begun, gradually, to take me over as I wrestled with creating all the different characters of my *Boğazkesen*, poring over a blank sheet of paper and lost in my own world of words; I had distanced myself from everyday life.

As I sat on the ferry, these houses passed before my eyes as if in a film, and so did the

The Beyazit tower, which, according to some guide books, 'is of no particular interest', is nevertheless one of Istanbul's symbols. It stands in the middle of the university gardens, where it was built to maintain a lookout for the fires that so often afflicted the city in the nineteenth century. Today you can look down from the tower over the Sea of Marmara, over the domes and minarets of the Beyazit Mosque, and gaze across to Mount Olympus, which can, on sunny days, be seen in the distance (opposite page). Leander's Tower, which has been a source of numerous legends since Byzantine days, stands at the mouth of the Bosporus, of which it has become the symbol. It has served successively as a lighthouse, a signal tower, a quarantine depot, a customs post and a club for Navy officers. Last summer, a group of young poets went there and proclaimed the Republic of Poetry, and proposed to the Mayor of Istanbul that it should be married with the Galata Tower (above).

There are many tea rooms in Istanbul, but only a few enjoy the designation of tea 'pavilion'. This is perhaps because 'pavilions' are not so frequented, like the one below at Çamlıca on the Asian side, built in the rococo style at the end of the last century. From the top of the tree-lined hill in Çamlıca one can admire the charm of the European shore (below). The dome of the Süleymaniye, Sinan's

masterpiece, towers majestically over the entrance to the Golden Horn and the Galata Bridge (opposite page). 'He conquered the world and made eighteen monarchs his subjects. He established order and justice in his territories, strode victoriously into the four quarters of the world, beautified the countries that he had subdued by force of arms and was successful in all his enterprises.' Thus wrote Evliya Çelebi, speaking of Sultan Süleyman, whom the Turks knew as 'the Legislator' and who was one of the few monogamous sultans. The beauty and cunning of his wife Hürrem (Roxelana) might have had a something to do with that.

people and objects that lived in them, and the streets, with the crowds and vehicles that filled them, and even the sky . . . these unfamiliar, or rather half-forgotten, images were making me feel somehow uneasy.

When I disembarked to mingle with the crowds at Eminönü, this feeling intensified. I was not an inhabitant of this city. I could not allow myself to be swept along all day, like them, in the bustling hurly-burly of this city. It was as if I had hit a mine, or run into another ship and sunk. I had lost all my bearings; I was defenceless. My only object, my only reason for being in this city was *Boğazkesen*. I had put together all the documents, notes and historical accounts that I needed in order to write my book. They were arranged neatly on shelves in the room with the corbelled window and were patiently awaiting the day when they would metamorphose into a story and shape the destiny of the story's characters.

As I thought about the other books which were going to inspire my own, in particular the old manuscripts, I felt somehow more relaxed. Before, I used to walk as the fancy took me, through the city, sitting in cafés at the water's edge, enjoying the cool evening air, or under the shade of plane trees at midday, or I would go to the small café where we used to arrange to meet before embarking on an evening's drinking; I thought I knew every street and every corner of this city. It was in the course of these peregrinations around Istanbul that I discovered the old houses. And it was on another occasion, during one of these solitary wanderings, that I went down into the Byzantine water cisterns and sat in the damp, musty cellars of Galata.

I had spoken of Istanbul in many of my books. I had expressed a nostalgia felt for Istanbul from a distance. The city of my imagination and the years of my adolescence. The city as mapped by historians and pictured by travellers. I had contrived to describe the streets of the city as well as its wooden buildings, the big hotels as well as its palaces. I could speak with equal facility of its mosques and of its churches and synagogues. Let us say that in the books which I had written up until then, a subjective image of Istanbul had set down its roots, with its own history and its own geography. An image without actors, which was distant but colourful. Colourful and real. Suddenly I realized that, in writing *Boğazkesen*, I was about to repeat all that, but in a different form. I had to find a system to express the historical dimension of the story while at the same time postponing the realities of history.

I hailed a cab and told the driver to drop me at the Fatih library. As we threaded through the crowds and the traffic in the streets of Eminönü, we arrived at Unkapanı, and went from there, via Saraçhane to Fatih. As I entered the library, I left behind me the noise of the city, the animal energy of the crowd, the incessant movement of buses and taxis, of the ships and ferries on the Bosporus, of the pigeons and seagulls. I left everything behind, all that chaos that was so much the opposite of the absence of life in a *yalı* in Anadolu Hisar, even my own movements, which belonged to that never-ending flux. And as I turned the dusty, well-worn pages of a manuscript, I suddenly understood the overwhelming immensity of Istanbul, and decided that I was never going to write *Boğazkesen* after all.

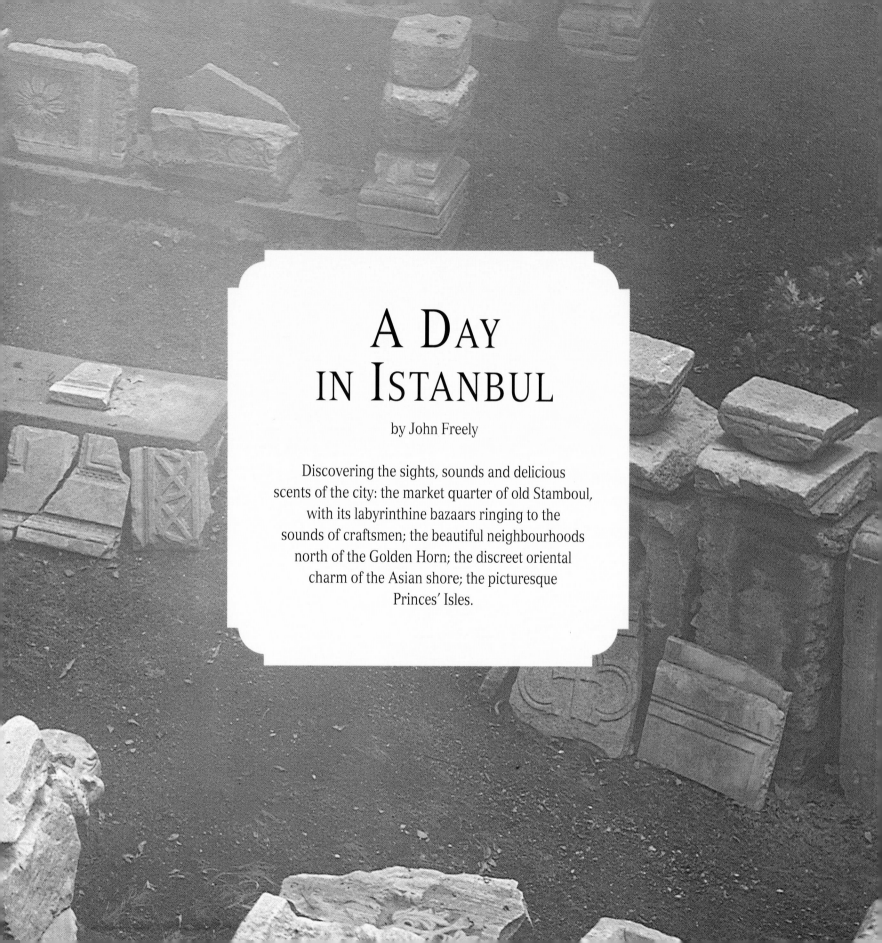

A Day
in Istanbul

by John Freely

Discovering the sights, sounds and delicious
scents of the city: the market quarter of old Stamboul,
with its labyrinthine bazaars ringing to the
sounds of craftsmen; the beautiful neighbourhoods
north of the Golden Horn; the discreet oriental
charm of the Asian shore; the picturesque
Princes' Isles.

Fragments of Greek and Roman antiquities provide a grandiose setting for the café opposite the Archaeological Museum (preceding double page). In the heart of the Süleymaniye mosque complex (*külliye*) can be heard the gentle murmer of the purifying waters spurting from the *şadırvan*, or ablution fountain (right). The *külliye* comprises, apart from the mosque itself, four *medrese* (theology schools), a preparatory school, an elementary school, a school for reading the Koran, a hospital, a soup kitchen, a caravanserai, a market, a *hamam*, and the mausolea of Süleyman and his wife Roxelana, as well as the tomb of Sinan, the mosque's architect. This gilded calligraphic inscription records the name of the founder and the date of the monument in a poetic chronogram (below). Beneath the domes of this *medrese* (opposite) are the cells of the students who came not only to study but also to live at the Süleymaniye.

Istanbul is the only city in the world that stands astride Europe and Asia, with its civic area stretching along both sides of the Bosporus from the Sea of Marmara to within sight of the Black Sea. The European part of the city is further divided by the Golden Horn, which enters the Bosporus about two kilometres from where it flows into the Sea of Marmara. The oldest part of the city, the great triangular peninsula that comprised Byzantine Constantinople, is on the south side of the Golden Horn, bound to the south by the Marmara and on its landward side by the ancient Theodosian walls. On the northern side of the Golden Horn, at the point where it enters the Bosporus, is the port quarter of Galata, which in the later Byzantine centuries was an independent city state under the aegis of Genoa. On the heights above Galata is the district known as Pera in Ottoman times, when it was the European quarter of the city, and which today is called Beyoğlu. Situated to the north of Beyoğlu, above the Bosporus, are the more modern neighbourhoods. Across the strait on the Asian side of the Bosporus is Üsküdar, a city in its own right for two thousand

The Süleymaniye, designed by Sinan, Chief of the Imperial Architects, and built between 1550 and 1557 for Süleyman the Magnificent, dominates the ridge above the Golden Horn. The smaller mosque on the shore, built in 1561, was designed by Sinan for Rüstem Paşa, Süleyman's Grand Vizier and son-in-law. The minor details in these Ottoman edifices are grace notes that add a human touch to the grandiose architectural theme, such as the foot-worn threshold in the gateway and the ogee-arched niche in the wall (below).

The houses of the old neighbourhoods along the south shore of the Golden Horn are perched on the slopes of the ridge that links six of the city's seven hills. The narrow cobbled streets are festooned with drying laundry, while groups of women cluster around the pedlars doing the rounds with their horse-drawn wagons and wicker baskets (above). The Fener quarter of the city is dominated by the Megali Scholion, or Great School, a secular institution of higher education for Greeks, built in 1881 (right).

years and now a suburb of Istanbul. Beyond Üsküdar, to the south-east off the Asian coast, are the Princes' Isles, Istanbul's southern archipelago in the Marmara. Thus Istanbul is half a dozen different cities, divided by what the Byzantine poet Procopius fourteen centuries ago called the city's 'garland of waters'.

Stamboul, the old city, includes within its boundaries seven hills. The first of these comprises the acropolis at the confluence of the Bosporus and the Golden Horn, where the ancient Greek city of Byzantium was founded in around 660 BC. The next five hills rise to form the long ridge that extends along the northern shore of the Constantinopolitan peninsula above

the Golden Horn, while the seventh rises to a peak off the south-western part of the city, near where the Theodosian walls come down to the Marmara. None of the hills is very high and their outlines have been obscured by all the buildings that have been erected on and around them, but they still constitute convenient landmarks when strolling around Stamboul.

The best place to begin a walk is the Galata Bridge, which crosses the Golden Horn between Karaköy in Galata and Eminönü in Stamboul, where the most colourful markets in the city are located. Fleets of ferries steam back and forth across the horn, whistling shrilly as they come and go, dodging one another in the swirling

A street scene in Unkapani on the south side of the Golden Horn. Here, as elsewhere in the poorer neighbourhoods of the old city, the streets are alive with swarms of lively children. Their street games are much the same as those that passing tourists may remember from their own childhoods in Paris, London or New York. The pedlars in these quarters tend to specialize in sweets, wafers and inexpensive toys. When they appear, the children cluster around, crying out to their mothers in the windows above to throw down a few coins for a treat.

A chimney-studded view from the roof of an old Ottoman *han* (left), one of the huge caravanserais that line the streets of the market quarter between the Covered Bazaar and the Golden Horn. Stallholders and passers-by still use the water from this eighteenth-century baroque fountain beside the Egyptian Market by the Galata Bridge (below).

Many of the old Ottoman fountains of Istanbul still serve the city's poor, who often do not have running water in their houses. A woman draws water from a rococo fountain in Yıldız Park (above), the now wooded grounds of a nineteenth-century Ottoman palace above the European shore of the lower Bosporus. Another woman fills her pitcher at a monumental eighteenth-century street fountain in Beykoz, a large village on the Asian shore (right).

waters. Silver and grey fish in large red tubs are sold by fishermen along the quay, who fry them up and slap them between two halves of a loaf of bread for hungry passers-by eating on the run. Pedlars hawk their wares above the din of the passing crowd, selling umbrellas when dark clouds threaten and sunglasses when it clears. When we see them carrying stovepipes we know that winter is drawing near.

The centre of the market quarter in Eminönü is behind and to the right of Yeni Camii, the New Mosque, which, despite its name, has dominated this area for nearly four centuries—such is the antiquity of Istanbul. In the garden behind the mosque, practitioners of some of the oldest trades in Istanbul can be seen: inscribers of seals and talismans; sellers of medicinal leeches; pedlars of perfume essences; fortune-tellers with divinatory rabbits; and professional 'petitioners', who write letters and fill out forms for illiterate peasants. All of these trades were once guilds and date back to Ottoman and Byzantine times. The very same shops and mosque courtyards have been used by successive generations of tradesmen since time immemorial. These ancient trades were described by Evliya Çelebi, a seventeenth-century Turkish chronicler, who spent his life writing a description of the Ottoman world of his time in a vast work called the *Seyahatname*, or Narrative of Travels. The most interesting part of this work is Evliya's description of the Procession of the Guilds that took place in Istanbul in 1638, during the reign of Murat IV. Evliya tells us that the procession consisted 'of all the Guilds and Professions, Merchants and Artisans, Shops and Various Occupations in the vast town of Constantinople', all of them, according to his lively description,

putting on shows to amuse and amaze the Sultan.

Among the merchants in the Procession of the Guilds described by Evliya were those of the Spice Bazaar: 'The Egyptian Grocers pass armed on wagons filled with baskets of ginger, pepper, cardamum, cinnamon, cloves, rhubarb, spikenard and aloes, forming altogether three thousand items.' Some three and a half centuries later, the handsome L-shaped building housing the Spice Bazaar can still be seen to the right of Yeni Camii. The Spice Bazaar, or Mısır Çarşısı (Egyptian Market) to call it by its proper name, is a veritable museum of eastern smells, featuring odoriferous herbs, gums, curative drugs, balms, unguents, spices, perfumes, incense and even an aphrodisiac advertised as 'the Sultan's Favourite'. It is as if all of the aro-

A colourful door in Istiniye on the European shore (below). Istiniye, the ancient Sosthenion, is the most deeply indented bay on the Bosporus. It has been a port since antiquity and was mentioned by Apollonius of Rhodes in his account of the voyage of Jason and the Argonauts. Up until recently, it was disfigured by large, floating dry docks, but these have been removed and

Istiniye is now one of the most attractive bays on the Bosporus. A seller of fishing gear in Çengelköy on the Asian shore (left). Çengelköy and all of the other communities along the Bosporus were originally fishing villages. Indeed, the rich fishing grounds of the strait were one of the reasons why Byzantium was founded. In recent years, this tradition has been revived and both banks are now crowded with anglers who cast their lines not only for sport but also to supplement the often meagre contents of their larders.

A man performs his ritual ablutions at the *şadırvan* in the mosque complex of Kiliç Ali Paşa in Tophane on the European shore (opposite page).
A child at a window in Fener, on the south bank of the Golden Horn (left). Istanbulites like to sit out in the street chatting or meditating. These two cheerful men are sitting in an alley in Beyoğlu (below left).
Garlic bulbs hung outside a door in the old city (below). There is an old Turkish tradition that when Satan first set foot on earth, onions sprang up from his right foot and garlic from his left foot. Thus garlic is sometimes used as a talisman to drive away evil, though the housewife who has hung this bundle up may not be aware of why she has done so—if asked she would probably say that it is an old tradition.

matic lands of Asia had concentrated their most exotic odours here under one roof to introduce the traveller to the heady atmosphere of the Orient. The Spice Bazaar is also famous for its coffee shops. They have been doing business here since coffee was first introduced to Europe from Turkey in the early seventeenth century, adding their pungent aroma to the odours of the spices.

Evliya also describes the display put on by the fishermen in the Procession of the Guilds: 'The fishermen adorn their shops on litters with many thousand fish, among which many monsters of the sea are to be seen. They exhibit dolphins on chains, sea horses, walruses, whales and other kinds of fish of great size, which they catch a couple of days before the procession and load onto wagons drawn by seventy-eight buffaloes.' The market Evliya alludes to is the city's oldest market for fish, fruit and vegetables, a small remnant of which survives today. The market was established here on the banks of the Golden Horn in late Roman times and was still in existence up until the late 1960s.

A gentleman relaxes with his hookah in an outdoor café in the Ali Paşa passage in Eminönü, in the market quarter near the Galata Bridge (above). Glasses of *çay* (tea) on a *tepsi*, a traditional Turkish tray (below right). Tea is cultivated in the Rize province by the Black Sea in north-eastern Turkey. It is always served in these pretty, bell-shaped glasses, along with one or two sugar lumps to soften its sometimes harsh flavour.

The principal flower market of the city is located in the garden enclosed by the L of the Spice Bazaar, adding its perfumed scents to the less subtle odours of the fish market. This market was also here in Evliya's day, and he describes the show that its merchants put on in the Procession of the Guilds: 'At the shops of these Flower Merchants in all seasons of the year are found dishes full of fruits and flowers, which are offered as presents to the viziers and great men. They make a great show in the procession, being an exquisitely armed troop.'

A section of the flower market contains shops selling tropical fish, birds and small animals, the most popular being goldfish, canaries

and other songbirds, parrots, rabbits and the occasional monkey. Caged nightingales are sometimes sold here, and children have been known to buy them just to set them free. Evliya tells us that in his day there were five hundred

A *bakkal* (grocery) in Unkapanı, with stacks of freshly baked *ekmek* (bread). This type of loaf is called *franjilah*, or 'French bread', as distinct from *pide*, or unleavened flat bread, which is sold during the sacred month of Ramadan (left).
A cartful of traditional Turkish sweets resembling crullers (above).

A dish of almonds served on a cake of ice. The combination is practical as well as delicious, because the ice makes the shells easier to remove (right). This fisherman's stall offers a meal in the street (below). A *bademci*, or almond seller, at an outdoor restaurant in the Galatasaray market (below right). Turkish market stallholders always take great pride in the artistry with which they display their wares. Their stalls add greatly to the pleasure of shopping in Istanbul. These carefully arranged green plums at the Galatasaray market are only sold for a 20-day period every year. Juicy and acidic, they are eaten with salt (opposite page).

nightingale merchants in Stamboul, noting: 'They furnish great men and barber shops with nightingales, which by their melodies enrapture the soul.'

On the slope of the First Hill which leads down from the Blue Mosque to the Marmara shore is one of the most picturesque quarters of Istanbul. Here one finds some of the most bizarre street names in the city, byways such as the Street of the White Moustache, the Avenue of the Bushy Beard, the Street of the Black Eunuch's Castle, and the Street of Ibrahim of Black Hell. The focal point of this old neighbourhood is Akbıyık Meydanı, the Square of the White Moustache, which has at its centre two beautiful old Ottoman fountains (*çesmes*), both dating from the mid-eighteenth century. There are some seven hundred of these Ottoman fountains still standing in Istanbul, most of them adorned with beautiful floral motifs and calligraphic inscriptions. Their presence in the old lanes and courtyards of the city evoke the atmosphere of a more gracious Ottoman past.

This old neighbourhood which lies below the Blue Mosque is separated from the Marmara shore by the ancient sea walls of Byzantine Constantinople. From the Square of the White Moustache one passes through the walls via Ahır Kapı, the Stable Gate, so called because the royal stables were located there in Byzantine and Ottoman times. Just beyond the gate to the left is an old restaurant known as Karismasen, which means 'Mind your own business!'— always good advice when dining in out-of-the-way places such as this.

On the summit of the Third Hill, next to the outer courtyard of the Beyazıdiye, the great mosque complex of Beyazıt I, there is a large square that was until recently the site of Istanbul's flea market, the Bit Pazar. The people of Stamboul still gather here in their thousands to buy and sell, just as they did in Evliya's day, as he writes in his description of the outer courtyard of the Beyazıdiye: 'The court has six gates and is adorned with lofty trees, under the shade of which many thousands of people gain a livelihood by selling various kinds of things.' Adjoining the outer courtyard of the Beyazıdiye is the Sahaflar Çarşisi, the second-hand book market, a picturesque courtyard lined with bookshops that have been doing business here since the beginning of the eighteenth century.

North of the Beyazıdiye, on the slope of the Third Hill leading down to the Golden Horn, is the famous Kapalı Çarşı, the Covered Bazaar, the largest and most interesting market in the Islamic world. The oldest of the buildings around the Kapalı Çarşı are the *hans*, huge commercial structures built as caravanserais in the early Ottoman centuries and still functioning today. The most colourful of these is the Valide Han, built in around 1650 by the Sultana Valide Kösem, wife of Ahmet I and mother of Sultans Murat IV and Ibrahim. Its main courtyard is a vast area 55 metres square, surrounded by a two-tiered arcade, with a tunnel leading to a sunken inner courtyard. The labyrinthine chambers of the inner courtyard are given over to every conceivable form of industry and commerce, the principal products of which appear

to be deafening noise and noxious chemical odours. The oldest of the *hans* is a block farther down the hill in the Mahmut Paşa quarter, with its entrance on Uzunçarsi Caddesi, the Avenue of the Long Market. This is the Kürkcü Hani, the Han of the Furriers, built soon after the Turkish conquest of Constantinople in 1453 and where the principal shops are still run by furriers. Evliya tells us that in his day these merchants were all Greeks who marched in the Procession of the Guilds dressed up in their furs as wild animals.

The shoreline of the Golden Horn below the Fourth, Fifth and Sixth Hills comprises some of the oldest residential quarters in the city. Up until half a century ago some of them were

The door of an old stone house in Çengelköy, one of the most picturesque villages on the Asian coast. Many of the wooden houses in Çengelköy date from the Ottoman Empire, recalling the tranquil atmosphere of the Istanbul of old (opposite page). These men are playing cards and drinking tea in the shade at an outdoor café, and practising *keyif*, the art of enjoying life to the full (above).

On a wall of the Şark Kafesi, a traditional Turkish café in the Covered Bazaar (right), is a portrait of Nasrettin Hoca. Usually portrayed mounted on his donkey, Nasrettin Hoca is a Turkish sage who lived in Anatolia in the thirteenth century. He composed a wealth of witty maxims—there seems to be one for every occasion—and Turks are never at a loss for funny stories about him. For example, the gate in front of his tomb in Aksehir is locked, but there is no fence or wall connected to it, so all those who approach Hoca's tomb have a smile on their lips. Shop selling objects made from copper and bronze in the *bedesten*, the heart of the Covered Bazaar where the most precious merchandise is sold (below). A typical scene in the Covered Bazaar, one of the most extraordinary markets in the world (below right). The babouches (*terlik*), worn by Turkish women at home, are always colourful and highly decorative, as if to compensate for the drab clothing which they wear outdoors (opposite page).

inhabited largely by minorities, with the Greeks predominating in Fener, Sephardic Jews in Balat, and Armenians living in both neighbourhoods, as well as in Kumpakı, an ancient fishing port on the shore of the Marmara that has some of the best fish restaurants in the city.

There is also an ancient Gypsy village at Sulukule, just inside the Theodosian walls, in the valley between the Sixth and Seventh Hills. The Gypsies have been living here since the late thirteenth century, when Emperor Andronicus II Palaeologus hired them as gamekeepers in the imperial preserve which lay just outside the city walls. Living with them in their village are a number of the dancing bears that the Gypsies lead about town, one of the many irregular occupations that have kept them in trouble with the police of the city for more than seven centuries. Evliya describes how the Gypsies

marched as a group in the imperial procession of 1638, taking first place among the 'Fools and Mimics' of Istanbul.

The slope of the Seventh Hill leading down

to the Marmara was known up until recent years as Samatya, a name referred to as far back as the fifth century BC, when it was a fishing port outside the walls of Byzantium. It is the oldest residential quarter of the city, and there are still significant numbers of Greeks and Armenians among the now predominantly Turkish population. In this lovely old quarter one still sees some of the old-fashioned street vendors who have now all but vanished from the more modern districts north of the Golden Horn. Each pedlar has his own distinctive cry, such as the long resonant call of the seller of *boza*, the favourite drink of the Janissaries. In Samatya one occasionally sees an old seller of *macun*, a multicoloured sweet paste, who advertises his wares to the children of his quarter in song: 'Weep, children, weep/Weep so your mother will buy you *macun!*'

The most important Moslem shrine in Istanbul is at Eyüp, a village which lies outside the Theodosian walls on the upper reaches of the Golden Horn. It is served by ferries that leave from the Stamboul shore just above the Galata Bridge. The shrine is named after Eba Eyüp, friend and standard-bearer of the Prophet Mohammed, who was killed in the first Arab siege of Constantinople in 674-678. Among those who pray at Eyüp's tomb are young boys dressed in festive costumes, making a pilgrimage here following their circumcision.

Above the village of Eyüp there is an exceptionally picturesque Moslem graveyard dating back to the time of the Conquest, with beautiful old Turkish tombstones, topped by turbans if the deceased was a man, or adorned with floral reliefs in the case of a woman. The epitaphs of the men are often witty and poetic, such as this

A market street between the Covered Bazaar and the Egyptian Market (opposite page). The porters (*hamal*) who unload the lorries and carry enormous loads down the narrow streets and alleyways are nicknamed camels. They are indispensable, for in order to get the merchandise into the depths of the old *han*, the *hamal* have to negotiate steps and streets which are too steep for vehicles.
Shaded by foliage, the Sahaflar Çarşsı, the second-hand book market, is a haven of cool and tranquility in the noisy bustle of the area around the Beyazıdiye mosque complex (above and left).

The Mısır Çarşsı, or Egyptian Market, better known as the Spice Bazaar, was founded in the early seventeenth century to sell goods imported from Cairo. The coffee-roasting establishment of Mehmet Efendi and Son, 'suppliers of the finest Turkish coffee since 1871', is particularly charming. The coffees are packaged on the spot in the heart of the market. In these colourful shops (opposite page), where stacks of bottles, jars and bags release the most delightful odours, one can buy, in addition to spices and dried fruits of all kinds, honey, cakes and *sahlep*—orchid bulbs in the form of a white powder, which is very expensive when bought pure and is used to make a delicious milky drink.

one on a wayside tomb: 'I could have died just as well without a doctor as with that quack that friends set upon me.'

At the top of the graveyard there is an old café known as the Teahouse of Pierre Loti, because it used to be frequented by the French writer during his years in Istanbul. The view from the teahouse is particularly romantic at sunset, when the turbaned tombstones and spectral cypresses of the cemetery are silhouetted against the glowing scimitar of the Golden Horn, whose lambent waters do indeed turn golden in the refracted light of the setting sun.

Near the Karaköy end of the Galata Bridge signs point the way to the lower terminus of the Tünel, the funicular railway built in 1874 to carry passengers from Galata up to Pera, now known as Beyoğlu. The main avenue in Beyoğlu, Istiklal Caddesi, begins at the upper terminus of the Tünel. The old tramway which runs the length of the avenue has recently been restored to service, taking passengers from the Tünel to Taksim Square, stopping halfway along the route at Galatasaray Square. In times past the avenue

was known as the Grand-Rue de Pera. It was flanked by the mansions that served as the embassies of the European powers and the homes of affluent people from the minorities of the Ottoman Empire, including Greeks, Armenians, Sephardic Jews and Levantine Europeans, whose numbers have decreased considerably over the past fifty years.

The first street to the right off Istiklal Caddesi beyond the Tünel leads to the Galata Mevlevi Tekke, or dervish monastery, founded in 1492. The centre of the *tekke* is the *semahane*, or dancing-room, where the Mevlevi performed the mystical dance, to the haunting music of the *ney*, or Turkish flute, that made them famous in Europe as the whirling dervishes. During Ottoman times there were scores of these *tekkes* in Istanbul, but now only this one remains open to the public, reminding us of what the city was like in the days of the dervishes.

The second street leading off to the left from Istiklal Caddesi after Galatasaray Square is given over to the colourful Galatasaray fish market. Just off Istiklal, next to the fish market, is the famous Çiçek Pasajı, or Flower Arcade, an L-shaped alleyway under a glass arcade. The alleyway is flanked by a score of lively *meyhanes*, or taverns, housed on the ground floor of a once elegant apartment block built in 1876. The Pasajı was restored a decade ago and cleaned up for the tourist trade, and most of the raffish characters who once congregated there—beggars, pimps, acrobats, wandering minstrels, pedlars, bums and petty criminals—are no longer allowed to enter, except for two strolling musicians, one of them a blind man who sings and plays beautiful music in the classical Ottoman style.

An old mansion in Fener, the neighbourhood on the south bank of the Golden Horn that was once the principal Greek quarter of Istanbul (above).
An ornate barber shop, which belongs to Muzaffer Bey, in Kuzguncuk, a charming village on the Asian shore of the lower Bosporus (below). Kuzguncuk is reminiscent of what Istanbul was like at the time of the Ottoman Empire. The inhabitants of this village have always lived together in harmony, no matter what their race or religion, which is why, a few yards from Muzaffer Bey's shop, stand a Turkish mosque, a Greek church, an Armenian church and a synagogue.

There are a number of good bars along the Istiklal Caddesi between Galatasaray Square and Taksim Square, the best being Café Pub and Papyrus, both of which are much frequented by Istanbul's writers and stage actors, as well as people working in the Turkish film industry, which is based in the labyrinthine streets just to the left of the avenue. This is the heart of Beyoğlu, the old Pera, which ends at the feature-less Taksim Square. Cumhuriyet Caddesi leads north from Taksim Square to the more modern districts of the town: Harbiye, Şişli, Maçka and Nişantası. One of the side streets on the left off Cumhuriyet Caddesi leads down to Kurtulus, an old neighbourhood where a few Greek tavernas have preserved the atmosphere of the Pera of times long past.

There are frequent ferries to Üsküdar on the Asian side from Eminönü and Kabataş, as well as smaller water taxis which make the crossing once they have filled up with passengers. The streets of Üsküdar are more redolent of the Turkey of old than the European part of Istanbul, for most of the people here are recent arrivals from Anatolia, many of them living in wooden Ottoman houses that have all but disappeared in other parts of the city. The main avenue that heads inland from the ferry landing leads uphill to the cemetery of Karaca Ahmet, the largest burial ground in Turkey, with some of its turbaned tombstones dating back to the fifteenth century.

Above Üsküdar is Büyük Çamlíca, the Great Hill of Pines, the highest summit in the vicinity of the river. The belvedere in the park there offers a magnificent panorama of the lower Bosporus and the imperial city across the strait.

Ferries leave from both Üsküdar and Eminönü for the Princes' Isles, with the express boats taking about an hour to reach the last stop. The little archipelago consists of nine islands, four of them substantial in size and permanently populated, the others tiny and inhabited, if at all, only in summer. The ferry stops at the four larger islands: Kınalı, Burgaz, Heybeli and Büyükada (Prinkipo in Greek), which is the largest and most famous. Despite their proximity to the city, the islands are still relatively unspoilt, and with their picturesque old wooden mansions they retain something of the charming atmosphere of the last days of the Ottoman Empire. Büyükada is still the most beautiful of the islands, particularly in spring when wisteria and bougainvillea vines envelop the fragile old mansions and Judas trees blossom pink and purple on the island's two hills. Above, great flights of storks spiral down to their ancestral nesting places on Mount Ayios Yorgios (Saint George) and nightingales serenade one another on moonlit nights. The view from the summit of Mount Ayios Yorgios is superb, with all of the Princes' Isles spread out below to the west off the Marmara shore. On a clear day you can also see, lying far beyond the isles on the horizon, the domes and minarets of Istanbul, the incomparable imperial city.

A late Ottoman building on Istiklal Caddesi, the main avenue in Beyoğlu (left). In late Ottoman times the avenue was known as the Grand-Rue de Pera and was lined with the embassies of the great European powers, now demoted to the status of consulates.

A rose window in Sirkeci Station, built as the terminus of the famous Orient Express, which made its first run through to Istanbul in 1888.

Büyükada, the Great Island, is the largest of the Princes' Isles, Istanbul's suburban archipelago off the Asian coast in the Sea of Marmara. Cars are not permitted on the isles and virtually all vehicles are horse-drawn. The taxis are phaetons, the beautiful old coaches that have now vanished elsewhere in Istanbul.

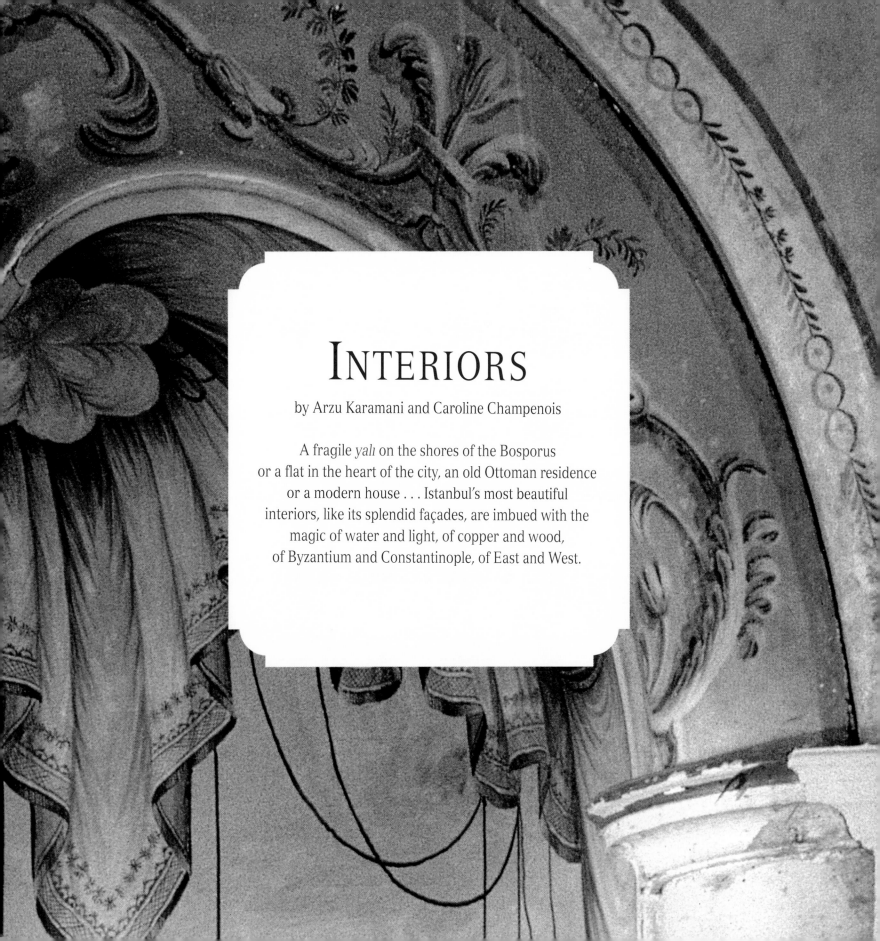

INTERIORS

by Arzu Karamani and Caroline Champenois

A fragile *yalı* on the shores of the Bosporus
or a flat in the heart of the city, an old Ottoman residence
or a modern house . . . Istanbul's most beautiful
interiors, like its splendid façades, are imbued with the
magic of water and light, of copper and wood,
of Byzantium and Constantinople, of East and West.

THE YALIS OF THE BOSPORUS

by Arzu Karamani

With every season, indeed with every hour of the day, the contours, colours and smells of the Bosporus change. When you look across from one shore to the other you have the sense of being by a river, but the seagulls and the large ships remind you that this is really the sea. In winter, when the mist descends, the two shores vanish completely. In summer the sun glistens on waters of the deepest blue. On some days you can smell the scent of jasmine and roses and on others the salty tang of sea air.

For over a hundred years the *yalıs*, like wooden ships at anchor, have witnessed this ever-changing spectacle. They were originally conceived as waterside summer residences and were built by the Ottoman aristocracy between the seventeenth and nineteenth centuries. Sandwiched conveniently between the cool shade of their gardens and the cool ocean breeze, their large airy rooms enabled their residents to escape from the stifling heat of the city.

No two *yalıs* are the same: they differ widely in their architecture, their ornamentation and the colours of their façades. Most of them, however, adhere to the same basic symmetrical layout, which is usually only altered in the event of an accident such as a fire. Two entrances—one from the sea, the other from the garden—open onto a cruciform central salon, the *sofa*, which is framed by four rooms, one at each corner. These are the bedrooms, or *oda*. This layout permitted the *yalı* to be divided into two sections: one for the women, the harem, and the other, the *selamlık*, for the men.

The word *yalı* comes from the Greek *yialos*, meaning seashore. To live in a *yalı* is, to all intents and purposes, to live with water, to invite the sea into your front room, to regard ships' sirens, the squawking of seagulls and the lapping of waves as the normal, everyday sounds of your home. But above all it is to live on a shoreline, and here on the Bosporus it is the shoreline of one continent facing the shoreline of another. It is, in short, to live on intimate terms, and on a daily basis, with the unique feature of Istanbul, the one that gives the city all its magic: the fact that it lies

A curtain rises on the magical world of the *yalıs*. Part of a *trompe l'œil* decorating a bedroom in the Sadullah Paşa *yalı* (preceding double page). The architecture of the Mocan *yalı*, with its pilotis and corbels, was greatly admired by Le Corbusier. Its pink façade follows a trend for pastel colours which started in the eighteenth century, replacing the traditional terracotta red (below). From the flower-decked, waterside terrace one can look across at the palaces on the European shore. The paving is a mosaic of black and white marble pebbles from Malta, arranged in floral motifs (opposite page).

The Mocan *yalı*, in common
with a number of *yalıs*, has
a cantilevered first floor,
supported by corbels (above).
The impact of its colour
is heightened by the contrast
with the black and white pebble
mosaic at the north entrance.
Behind the large windows of the
main entrance stands a
Venetian-style double staircase
(left). In the 'golden salon'
on the first floor, the rays of the
setting sun fall on light-coloured
fabrics and linger on an
armchair that seems to invite
you to sit and contemplate
the Bosporus (right).

The 'golden salon' is clearly the most European room in the Mocan *yalı*. The stencilled pattern on the walls is inspired by the Venetian decor of the ceiling, the curtains are English and the furniture French. The large eighteenth-century Uşak carpet, however, puts an Ottoman stamp on this room, which has something of the atmosphere of a cabin on an ocean liner.

between East and West, at the meeting point of two worlds.

THE MOCAN *YALI*. One *yalı* expresses this geographical and cultural encounter better than any other. Built in 1732 on the Asian shore by General Fethi Ahmet Paşa, it was given the name of Mocan in the twentieth century when it became the residence of one of his descendants, the politician Şevket Mocan. It is also called the Pink *yalı* because of its colour, which blends so well with the other pastel shades of the Bosporus. Located between the villages of Üsküdar and Kuzguncuk, it lies well below the road, hidden by cypresses and Judas trees, and

is only visible from the sea. Although a large section of the *yalı*, principally the harem, disappeared in a fire in 1920, the 20 remaining rooms still make it a splendid summer palace. The consoles which support the projecting first-floor rooms are its most striking feature. They look like giant arms holding the rooms up out of the water.

The present interior was designed by one of Şevket Mocan's daughters, Rüya Nebioğlu, an interior decorator who lives for part of the year in London. One of her main aims was to bring light and colour into rooms which she felt had always been stifled by their dark, heavy furnishings. Accordingly, she opted for

Rüya Nebioğlu's bedroom looks out onto the garden. As in the other rooms of the *yalı*, she has sought to combine European and Ottoman styles.

The large, pink Sarköy kilim decorated with floral motifs and the wooden chair inlaid with mother-of-pearl blend harmoniously with the room's English furniture (left).

This beautiful white marble fountain in the dining room, with its tiled surround and scallop-shaped dishes, dates from the eighteenth century (above).

It is at sunset that the 'golden salon' really justifies its name. A warm light suffuses the room, caressing the contours of this splendid Louis XV settee, and uniting the flowers on the nineteenth-century painting, the pouffe and the wallpaper (right). Kemal Atatürk, whose elegant, uniformed figure lurks behind one of the doors (above), keeps a benevolent eye on things.

fabrics, wallpaper, carpets, curtains and blinds in light colours with predominantly floral motifs. She also wanted the decor to remain true to the history and character of the Bosporus whilst at the same time reflecting

her own lifestyle, so she created a blend of European and Ottoman styles. In the large dining room, for example, a marble fountain decorated with eighteenth-century Kütahya tiles cohabits happily with seventeenth-century Portuguese chairs, and in the very English drawing room on the ground floor, the floor is spread with kilims.

By placing these two worlds side by side, Rüya Nebioğlu has succeeded in preserving the original spirit of the house. From its conception, the Mocan *yalı* was characterized by precisely this mixture of styles. Its first occupants had taken their cue from the sultans, whose Dolmabahçe Palace had drawn on a

Şevket Mocan's office has a fine inlaid parquet flooring and large windows which open onto the garden (above). A brass brazier catches the light of the sun (below left). For a long time these braziers were the only system of heating in the *yalıs* .

variety of different European styles. In the first-floor drawing room, the ceiling ornamentation, marquetry and parquet are the work of Venetian craftsmen who decorated the palace during the nineteenth century. Under the staircase in the main hall, decorated with Venetian-style, lyre-shaped balustrades, is a selection of finely sculpted wooden chairs that were imported from India in 1840.

The *sofa* of the Rahmi Koç *yalı*, built in 1895, houses a splendid collection of furniture and works of art. The traditional, ornate wooden structure encloses a small salon furnished with divans (above).

THE RAHMI KOÇ *YALI.* 'You absolutely must arrive by boat!' insisted Ömer Koç. He lives in one of the finest *yalıs* on the Bosporus, a white nineteenth-century residence situated in Anadoluhisari on the Asian shore. I am glad that I followed his advice, because when one approaches it from the sea, the *yalı* reveals its architectural details little by little—a pleasure that must have been all the greater for the Ottoman dignitaries of the past whose caïques travelled at a more leisurely pace.

Disembarking at a small jetty, one passes between the two lion statues that guard the house then enters through the main door of the *yalı*. On entering, one registers the tradi-

tional cruciform layout, and an atmosphere of calm and simplicity despite the opulent furnishings. The nineteenth-century European settees, the Chinese vases, the precious antique kilims, the collection of antique watercolours depicting Istanbul in the old days—all this is displayed with studied elegance. One stops to admire the objects one by one, pausing at the windows that look out onto the Bosporus and the Rumeli fortress on the opposite shore.

Rahmi Koç and his son Ömer are both knowledgeable collectors and each item has its own carefully chosen place in the house. Their collection of antique books, most of which are about Istanbul, was put together by Ömer. They are kept on the first floor, between the bedrooms and a private drawing room which have been decorated in a style that is at once warm and simple.

On the ground floor, the main drawing room opens onto a fine terraced garden. The low garden walls feature Roman and Byzantine gravestones, most of which were discovered during the excavation of the building's foundations.

There is also an impressive collection of amphorae, gathered discreetly in one corner, and, further along, a table made up of two sheets of glass placed on a pair of large rudders set side by side. All these treasures, which lie half-hidden in the greenery, demonstrate the interlinking of history and nature which has always been a feature of life in Istanbul. Finally, there is a charming vine arbour running along the bank were one can enjoy a drink with friends, ideally at sunset when the magnificent waters of the Bosporus are ablaze.

Like the *Palazzi* of Venice, Istanbul's earliest *yalıs* were built right at the water's edge (top), and in a sense their largest, brightest room is the Bosporus itself. The garden, cool and pleasantly scented, is another outdoor room. The garden of Rahmi and Ömer Koç contains a wealth of fascinating treasures (above). These Byzantine gravestones, for example, were discovered during the building of the *yalı* (left).

In this interior sobriety and refinement are the watchwords. The French settee in the drawing room that overlooks the Bosporus dates from the nineteenth century and the simplicity of its red upholstery offsets the multicoloured motifs of the kilim (above). To its left, a collection of Roman marble heads is displayed on a wooden cabinet painted in the 'Edirne' style (right).

THE *YALI* OF NURI BIRGI. When the inhabitants of Megara in Greece decided to abandon their barren land, they consulted the oracle at Delphi to find out where their new home might be. The oracle spoke of a country which was separated by a stretch of sea from the 'land of the blind'. This 'country' was the peninsula which would later see the building of the Topkapı Palace, Haghia Sophia and the Blue Mosque, a magnificent land which only blind people—those who inhabited the land on the other side of the strait—could possibly have missed choosing for themselves. Such is the legend of the origins of Istanbul.

Who would dare to suggest nowadays that this *yalı* is in the 'land of the blind'? Certainly no-one who has had a chance to visit it, or, even better, spend a few days there. Built at Salacak, at the top of a steep section of the Asian shore, it is one of the few *yalıs* not to have its feet in the water. One of its 20 windows which overlook the sea offers an extraordinary panorama of Istanbul, taking in the Sea of Marmara, the minarets of the mosques, Topkapı Palace and the Galata Bridge.

It is with a similar sense of wonder that one discovers the rest of the property. Over the years, Muharrem Nuri Birgi put together a fascinating collection of furniture and *objets d'art*. Of particular interest is the collection of Beykoz

Ömer Koç has a good eye for detail, as can be seen in this still life arrangement of a bronze rose and a terracotta vase on an eighteenth-century Italian console table.

In spring, the pink flowers of the Judas trees brighten the shores of the Bosporus. Eventually the flowers fall to the ground, forming a delicate carpet on which one hesitates to tread. In the garden of the Ambassador's *yalı,* the flowers are offset by the terracotta red of the building. The garden and the interior were designed by Nuri Birgi. In the *sofa* on the first floor, the pearl-grey walls harmonize perfectly with the mauve of the wisteria.

Selahattin Beyazit, the present owner of the Ambassador's *yalı*, has kept all the objects and furniture collected by Nuri Birgi. Concerts and receptions are given in the dining room on the ground floor (below and right), where

some of the finest treasures are displayed. These include Ottoman engravings, little porcelain leopards (above), which are cleverly matched with speckled shells, and Chinese, Danish and German ceramics. In the centre of the room stands a large nineteenth-century French dining table. In the sunlight of the Bosporus, this still life, with its small pears and a Bohemian glass carafe which is probably filled with lemonade, is a mouth-watering prospect (right).

glass, the Chinese ceramics and various watercolours and calligraphies. At every step one savours the interplay of light and shade provided by wooden shutters, which are open or closed depending on the weather. Outside, behind the *yalı*, the garden rambles in a studied disorder, in which Judas trees are reflected in small ornamental pools.

Muharrem Nuri Birgi was Turkey's ambassador to Britain, and ambassador to NATO in Brussels. He bought the *yalı* in 1968 and it was from that moment that it became known as the Ambassador's *yalı*. He restored it lovingly, on occasion retrieving items from other, ruined *yalıs*, and decorated it himself with impeccable taste. After his death, a friend of his—the businessman Selahattin Beyazit—became the new owner. He does not live in the *yalı*, but maintains it in a manner that respects its past. Over the years, a number of distinguished visitors have had the privilege of being received here, including Yehudi Menuhin, who played here, André Malraux, Rockefeller and Lord Carrington.

One of the finest *sofas* in one of the finest *yalıs* on the Bosporus, the Kıbrıslı *yalı*. Here the flowers, the stonework and the water bring the garden into the room. The pebble mosaic, the *şadirvan* (marble fountain), the *mangal* (large brazier), the *sedirs* (low divans) and the quality of the light make this *sofa* particularly delightful (left). The garden (above) is a mass of peonies, the fetish-flowers of the *yalıs*.

The archaeologist Selim Dirvana, great-grandson of Mehmet Paşa Kıbrıslı, is as solicitous in his care for his *yalı* as he is for his extensive family who share the place with him (above). In the aquatic magic of the *yalıs*, everything seems possible, even the thought of drinking a large glass of *raki* with black and white mulberries. *Raki* is generally accompanied by savoury titbits. When, as here, it is diluted with water—which turns it white—the Turks call it 'lion's milk' (right).

THE KIBRISLI *YALI*. If there is one *yalı* where one still feels the spirit of the past, it is the Kıbrıslı *yalı* at Kandilli. This white, broad-fronted *yalı* was built in 1775 on the slopes of Lover's Hill, with its covering of Judas trees. It is one of the largest *yalıs* and somehow resembles a pale young girl lying at the water's edge. It has a simple, traditional layout, in which the central section is framed by the harem on one side, and the *selamlık* (the men's apartments) on the other. Today it is inhabited by Selim Dirvana, the great-grandson of the original owner, Mehmet Paşa Kıbrıslı (the Cypriot), governor of Jerusalem and several times Grand Vizier. Mehmet Paşa Kıbrıslı was attract-

ed to this unique spot on the Bosporus: here the hillside turns at right angles to the sea, catching all the coolness of the sea breeze.

Selim Dirvana relishes speaking the Istanbul dialect and visiting the *yalı* in his company

94

The west drawing room of the *yalı* overlooks the garden on one side and the sea on the other (left). It was here that the Grand Vizier Mehmet Paşa Kıbrıslı received the Empress Eugénie of France. A portrait of Mehmet Paşa in the drawing room presides over a group of photographs of his descendants (above).

In the Sadullah Paşa *yalı* various tell-tale details, such as this eighteenth-century paper fan (below), reveal that the guiding spirit of the place is a woman. The woman in question is Aysegül Nadir, who has

overseen the magnificent restoration of the *yalı*. This *trompe l'œil* in one of the bedrooms is by the same artist who painted the *trompe l'œil* in Topkapı Palace. It depicts Küçüksu Palace and the Kıbrıslı *yalı* (right). The most striking feature on the first floor is the unusual, oval-shaped central *sofa*. The rays of the large sun at the centre of the dome are echoed on the eighteenth-century Uşak carpet below (opposite page).

is a pleasure. 'You must come back when the peonies are in flower,' he says, as he crosses the garden. 'They are the symbol of this house.' A few moments later, as we enter the large marble-paved *sofa* linking the interior with the garden and the sea beyond, we realize why: its arched ceiling is decorated with peony motifs. The *sofa* in the left wing has large windows which look out onto the garden. A soft light, filtered by the foliage, slides across a divan and settles on a mosaic made up of black and white pebbles arranged in floral motifs, which surrounds a marble basin.

Selim Dirvana leads us into the large reception room where the paşa used to give sumptuous feasts in honour of his illustrious guests. When the Empress Eugénie of France

visited the small neighbouring palace of Küçüksu, she had admired the *yalı*. Captivated by her charm, Mehmet Paşa Kıbrıslı invited her to dinner, and presented her with a rose, the petals of which concealed a diamond. Many years later the *yalı* was visited by another prestigious guest, the French writer Pierre Loti, who was staying in a very fine *yalı* nearby which belonged to Count Ostrorog.

Today a warm family atmosphere has replaced the grandeur of the past. A multi-coloured kite hangs from the ceiling and children's bicycles are propped against the old divans. The ancestors, whose portraits hang alongside a collection of contemporary paintings, seem to be wearing expressions of amusement as they look down on these scenes of domestic informality.

THE SADULLAH PAŞA *YALI*. If you travel by boat up the Bosporus towards the Black Sea, immediately after the magnificent Beylerbeyi Palace you will suddenly see a small *yalı* at the water's edge. It is a sober-looking building, painted red, and is curiously reminiscent of a doll's house. It is the Sadullah Paşa *yalı*, or at least what is left of it, for only the former harem remains. The building's simple façade conceals a sumptuous, baroque-influenced interior.

Sadullah Paşa, the original occupant of this eighteenth-century *yalı*, was Turkey's ambassador to Austria during the reign of Abdül Hamit II. The *yalı* was bought in 1982 by Asil Nadir and was completely restored by his wife Aysegül, who is an expert collector with a passion for Ottoman art. She is the presiding spirit of this enchanting *yalı*.

Meals at the Sadullah Paşa *yalı* are always taken in the dining room overlooking the Bosporus. The tableware includes pink plates that once belonged to an Egyptian princess, Russian crystal and delicately iridescent Roman glassware. The stylized carnations on the table cloth are a traditional Ottoman motif (left). Aysegül Nadir offers her guests magnificent Ottoman dishes, such as this elegantly served Circassian chicken (right).

On the other side of the room is a small Ottoman salon with its *sedirs* and, in the centre, a large copper tray on which is displayed a collection of small containers made of *tombak*, copper plated with an alloy of gold and mercury (above).

The large central *sofa* is surrounded by four bedrooms, one at each corner, and is unusual in that it is oval-shaped. The room has a domed ceiling which features a celestial sphere with the sun at its centre. A huge Uşak carpet, whose central medallion features a similar motif, gives the room the flavour of a nomad tent. The *sofa* is flanked by two smaller rooms containing divans, one positioned for watching the sea and the other overlooking the garden. Each of the square bedrooms has a niche decorated with a fresco similar to ones that can be seen in Topkapı Palace, which were painted by the same artist. This traditional layout—a central *sofa* surrounded by four bedrooms—is replicated on the ground floor. The two levels are joined by symmetrical staircases, one of which has a gallery which originally would have been designed for the use of musicians.

Aysegül Nadir has contrived to maintain the simplicity of the interior by furnishing and decorating it with exquisite taste. There are relatively few pieces of furniture, and each item is a wonder in itself. There are the eighteenth-century armchairs upholstered with Ottoman embroideries, the Turkish settees covered in Fortuny fabrics, and the sixteenth-century baroque table in gilded wood and marble. In addition, the walls are decorated with embroideries, sumptuous calligraphies, some of which are executed in gold thread, and antique engravings.

Even the appropriately named Magic, a fine grey Persian cat who follows you around miaowing during your visit, seems to be part of this fairy-tale world, which continues out in the garden, where Aysegül Nadir has a collection of Graeco-Roman marbles and antique earthenware jars. It is here that she likes to receive her many friends, on summer evenings, by candlelight. For people sailing down the Bosporus at night, the softly lit Sadullah Paşa *yalı* must look like a marvellous and enchanting mirage.

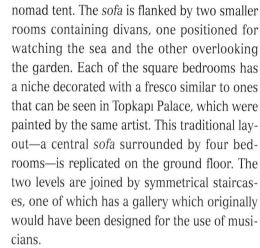

Audacious displays of works of art reinforce the magical atmosphere of the Sadullah Paşa *yalı*. Here, Greek and Roman sculptures are placed next to three *alems* on an eighteenth-century wooden table.

In the bedroom, the canopy bed, the prayer mat and the calligraphy are Ottoman. Only the chair, upholstered in a fabric featuring a design of *çintemani* motifs, is European (left). Numerous objects scattered about the house also contribute to its magic, such as this ivory-handled fly-whisk (above).

This large sultan's tent, where one can lounge on cushions while drinking coffee by candlelight, evokes the atmosphere of the *Thousand and One Nights*. It is erected during the summer season in the garden of the Sadullah Paşa *yalı* and is used for receptions.

THE ŞERIFLER *YALI*. Across the Bosporus, on the European shore, lies the Şerifler *yalı*. It was built in the Emirgân gardens during the seventeenth century and has undergone frequent demolition and reconstruction, changing hands many times. For a time it was owned by Şerif Abdullah Paşa, hence its name. In the nineteenth century, Ismail Paşa, Khedive of Egypt, laid out a fine garden here, including several pavilions and a number of elegant pools. The *yalı* lost its harem in 1940, due to the construction of the nearby road, and became the property of the state in 1966. It has now been successfully restored to its former splendour.

What first strikes you when you enter the large central salon is the light. The windows seem to usher in the bright daylight, which reflects off a white marble fountain. The tinkle of the fountain merges with the sound of the waves outside as you pause to study the richly decorated ceiling. It is made of red wood, decorated with floral motifs arranged around the delicately carved polychrome rays of a central sun. The whole ceiling is framed by a frieze of flowers that stand out distinctly against a black background and each corner is decorated with a naïve landscape of pavilions and gardens painted in delicate colours.

One finds this same naïve effect, this freshness, in the decorations on the walls of the

entrance hall: painted summerhouses framed in medallions; bouquets of flowers; garlands carved in wood; mellow, fruity colours depicting a universe that is almost childlike. One almost hesitates to open the doors that lead off

the hall, because, with their arabesques and flowers, they look so light that they might fly away.

The charm of the Şerifler *yalı* lies precisely in this naïve lightheartedness, a kind of decorative innocence which has permitted its owners to mix with impunity every style imaginable, from chinoiserie to baroque, from classical to rococo. This profusion of styles serves, perhaps, to compensate for the rigidity of the traditional cruciform layout which, despite the *yalı's* succession of different owners, is the only element to have remained unchanged since it was built during the eighteenth century.

The simplicity of the façade of the Sadullah Paşa *yalı* belies the sumptuousness of its interior (left). It is this contrast which is the source of its charm and its mystery. At sunset, a happy marriage of colours and materials brings grace and an element of the unexpected to this small quay, where one can sit and enjoy the cool of the evening (above).

Nowadays a road separates the Şerifler *yalı* from the shore of the Bosporus, but water is still present everywhere. All the windows of the reception room in the *selamlık* overlook the sea and an imposing white marble fountain stands in the centre (right). The simplicity of the *sedirs* serves to highlight the splendour of the ceilings, which are the most extraordinary feature of this *yalı* (right). In this ornate side-room (above) the marble hearth, with its polychrome wooden surround decorated with floral motifs, is typical of the astonishing mixture of styles that one finds in every room.

HOMES OF CHARM

———

by Caroline Champenois

For many Istanbulites Polonezköy, the Polish village, serves as a delightful weekend retreat, with its enchanting wooden houses tucked away in the greenery, Polish-style hospitality, and magnificent landscape of woods and valleys. Less than an hour from the city, the Polish village is like another world, an oasis of tranquility (below). Daniel Ohotski, a resident of Polish origin, has lovingly restored his house—the oldest in the village—and opens it to visitors. The bedroom has a rustic feel, with its bare beams and floorboards, its whitewashed walls and fine antique curtains. The house is filled with photographs of his ancestors, who seem to keep a watchful eye on things like guardians of the past (opposite page).

They may be houses or flats, made of wood or of stone, old or recent. You can find them right in the heart of Istanbul or out in the suburbs, in the country or by the sea. Yet wherever they might be, all of these homes have one thing in common: a distinct, almost palpable soul derived from the charm of a particular place and the people who live there. It is in the scent of old polished wood, the patina of years past which softens light and colour, the mysteries that hide in shadowy, forgotten corners and the curtains that billow in the Bosporus breeze. It is the charm of a place imbued with serenity, a place where time has stood still.

THE POLISH VILLAGE. Less than an hour's drive from Istanbul, in Asia, the wooden houses

of Polonezköy, the Polish village, possess this charm in abundance. The village was founded in the 1850s by Polish refugees who had fought in the Ottoman army during the Crimean war. It had no road until the start of this century and has only enjoyed electricity since 1973. Most of the present inhabitants are of Polish descent. They have maintained the traditions of their ancestors and live in old, single-storey wooden houses, where the balconies, wooden verandas, flower-filled gardens and picket fences transport us to a delightful Central European landscape that has remained unchanged for centuries.

The people of Istanbul have always enjoyed coming to Polonezköy for weekends. Even when the state of the roads meant that it took a half-day to get there, the delicious foods prepared by the Polish peasants made the journey worthwhile. Nowadays overstressed citizens come here to enjoy the tranquility of small lanes that wind across the hills, of long walks in the woods, and the ever-changing spectacle of the seasons with their carpets of autumn leaves or spring wild flowers. Some of the villagers let out rooms and offer meals to visitors and one of the greatest pleasures is to stay in one of their homes. Tucked away in the greenery, simple and welcoming, these peaceful houses offer an ideal break for anyone seeking to forget the feverish pace of Istanbul for a day or two.

The terrace in Daniel Ohotski's garden is a charming place in which to savour the pleasures of spring. Polonezköy has many spots like this—peaceful, shady and conducive to rest and relaxation (above). Daniel Ohotski's house was probably built in around 1860. For the refugees of that period, these small fences and verandas were familiar evocations of the typical country houses of their homeland (left). The house where Haldun Simavi spends his weekends, one of the largest in Polonezköy, is looked after by a woman from the village. It is reached by descending a large wooden staircase (right).

IN SEARCH OF TIME PAST. Göztepe, an outlying suburb of Istanbul on the Asian shore, is a place where artists come to live, drawn by its village atmosphere. On the ground floor of a modern block is a flat that looks as if it belongs in the nineteenth century. It is the home and work-place of Hakan Ezer, a young, fashionable interior designer and jewellery designer, a lover of the night, of travel and of things of the past. He has gone to great lengths to give his flat a patina of age. Anything modern is barred. The wood of the kitchen cupboards, for example, looked too new so he had it artificially aged. If a window happens to be square, it is magically transformed into an Ottoman-style window with the aid of a traditional curtain, like those that can be seen in the Beylerbeyi Palace. And when he makes a chair, he upholsters it with velvet that has been treated, or rather mistreated, to give it an aged look. It is not so much the past that fascinates Hakan Ezer as the way that the passing of time leaves its mark on things. In his view the traces it leaves are sacred. This explains the delightful effect he creates by using old things that are slightly worn and tattered, and the strange sensation one has of entering into a flat that has been left untouched, hidden behind a bricked-up door for years.

Hakan Ezer's preferred material is wood, because of the warmth and sense of history that it gives. His passion for wood is obvious from the furniture, flooring and woodwork in the living room, which he decorated himself. It can also be seen in the furniture which he has made, such as his drawing board, and two chairs in his sitting room, which are based on original designs by Josef Hoffmann.

Old books, trinkets from any period as long as they are not new, and souvenirs of foreign travels make up a theatrical decor in which the characters in the black-and-white family photographs, dotted about the room, act out a play, which is not without humour, about the absurdity and ephemerality of life.

Hakan Ezer has chosen only objects that are old and worn, creating an effect that is both nostalgic and surreal. Here he has juxtaposed a portrait of an Ottoman dignitary, some bars of soap and an old piece of wood from a *yalı* or *konak* (below).

This window has been aged a hundred years thanks to these nineteenth-century Ottoman curtains. Hakan Ezer makes everyday use of his collection of Turkish glassware, respectfully observing the traditional function of

each item. Nothing in his flat has outlived its usefulness; each object and piece of furniture continues to age through daily use (left). In the bathroom, an accumulation of period objects relating to the twin themes of water and bathing sums up the designer's approach, which is at once charming and unsettling (above).

For this passageway, Hakan Ezer has chosen a seat that came from another place of passage. The bench used to stand on a station platform in the Tünel, the underground railway built in 1875 (above). Even this telephone and these set squares, all in daily use, are old and charged with memories (left). Were it not for the many ironic touches, walking into Hakan Ezer's sitting room (right) would be a bit like entering the unopened tomb of some pharaoh. The clothing on the dressmaker's dummy, embroidered in the so-called 'European style', dates from the beginning of the century, as does the English settee covered in red velvet. The wooden grille, which once protected a window in some Ottoman house, is considerably older.

Living at the highest point in Istanbul offers rare pleasures: a view of the city and the sea stretching to the horizon, total peace and clean air. The house owned by antique dealer Yaman Mursaloğlu, with its large garden terrace, is reminiscent of the finest *yalıs*. Steps lead down from the garden to his subterranean office, a veritable Aladdin's cave packed with antiques and old books (below).

THE ÇAMLICA BELVEDERE. At 267 metres above sea level, Büyük Çamlıca, the Great Hill of Pines, is the highest point in Istanbul. Byzantine and Ottoman princes used to reserve this spot for themselves, coming here in summer to enjoy the country air. In around 1870 a palace was built here which was the home of the last heirs of the Ottoman empire. Its three distinct buildings—the main residence, the hunting lodge and the guard-house—are still today the only buildings on the pine-covered hillside. The antique dealer Yaman Mursaloğlu has the good fortune to live in the hunting lodge, where the layout and, in particular, the red façade are reminiscent of the *yalıs* along the coast of the Bosporus. His living room, his bedroom and his terrace all command extraordinary panoramic views over Istanbul and the Sea of Marmara, with the Princes' Isles visible in the far distance.

The hospitable Yaman Mursaloğlu has restored his hilltop palace with skill and taste. Proud of his country's past, he has assembled a fine collection of antiques. Unquestionably he is a prince who is worthy of his privilege.

The bathroom in Marmara marble is a miniature reconstruction of an old *hamam*. Its furnishings and fittings, which date mostly from the eighteenth century, include two carved fountains with their original brass taps,

a cupboard filled with traditionally embroidered towels, a small stool and a bowl (left). The mirror above the sink reflects a nineteenth-century engraving illustrating the delights of a harem as imagined by a western artist (above).

A Secret garden
in the Heart of the City

Istanbul. 5p.m. On the ground floor of a block of flats in Topağaci the muezzin's call is heard. Here the couturier Cemil Impekçi has transformed what was originally an ordinary courtyard into a secret garden. From May to October it also serves as an outdoor dining room. Guests are expected. The lace tablecloth is French, the chairs were made in Istanbul, and the large kilim is from Uzbekistan. Cemil Impekçi also designed the façade of his ground-floor flat, which is quite different from the rest of the building and was inspired by old Levantine houses in Pera. The pergola, with its roof of greenery, is also his creation. An Indian sari has been used for the curtain. Alexander the Great, of whom there are two plaster busts on the ground, copied from originals in the Archaeological Museum, would surely have loved this fairy-tale decor in which different cultures meet in a celebration of friendship.

A DERVISH FLAT. In 1990, Murat Morova decided to abandon his career as an interior designer to dedicate himself full-time to his principal passion, painting. He has transformed a flat in the Teşvikiye neighbourhood into a home, a studio and a place for meditation. Bare walls, sparse black furnishings and a white ceil-

Murat Morova's bedroom is monastic in its simplicity. The painter loves empty space, subdued lighting and traditional dervish artefacts (opposite page), which are an inspiration to him in his work.

ing create a space consistent with the paintings of an artist who has long had an interest in mysticism. It also matches Murat Morova himself, a man who chooses his words carefully and whose ascetic face lights up with a smile when he greets you. With warmth and simplicity he ushers you into a minimalist sitting room: a few simple cushions placed on the floor around a brass tray that serves as a low table, together with a few precious objects, including several antique guns. He serves you tea. At the other end of the room is one of the painter's recent works: a large triptych which seems to fill the room with its dark and vibrant surface.

Murat Morova's treatment of the walls in his flat involved simply scraping them almost bare, leaving only traces of their previous wall-coverings. 'These traces', the painter explains, 'make me think of all the people who have projected their thoughts and feelings onto these walls before me. To meditate between these four walls is, for me, a lesson in humility.'

In 1991 the artist was working on the theme of the Apocalypse and it was within this monastic decor that he read all the sacred books. Some evidence of this period of work remains in the flat, such as the icon of St Francis of Assisi on the floor by the bed. Today he gets his inspiration from the mystical tradition of Islam, drawing on the religious symbolism of colours and signs. His collection of Sufi objects—chains used in religious ceremonies by the Rufai sect, a dervish's hat embroidered with verses from the Koran, ostrich eggs that were reputed to keep spiders away, and a rhinoceros-horn cup—seem like mysterious souvenirs of a voyage: Murat Morova's voyage towards sacred truths.

In contrast to the fluid style of her paintings, Hale Arpacioğlu has chosen a decor of pure lines and contrasting geometric forms. Several pieces of Çanakkale pottery dating from the late nineteenth century have been arranged on this secretaire, together with an eighteenth-century Sufi calligraphy painted on wood (above).

AN ARTIST'S INTERIOR AT ARNAVUTKÖY. With its tall, narrow, traditional wooden houses, Arnavutköy is one of the most delightful villages on the European shore of the Bosporus. Artist Hale Arpacioğlu has created a duplex out of the top floor and roof terrace of one of these houses.

A former antique dealer, Hale Arpacioğlu had no difficulty in decorating her flat with old furniture and objects, which are interspersed with some of her own paintings. She describes her relationship with her kilims, Art Deco furniture, ceramics and paintings as one of 'love at first sight'. This love at first sight, however, almost certainly has an element of premedita-

tion. The rectangular shapes of tables and dressers, the circular forms of armchair backs, antique trays and lamp bulbs, and the diamond and triangle patterns of the kilims create a decor rich in pure geometric forms. They provide a striking contrast with the fluid lines in the paintings of this talented and sensitive artist who describes her work as following in the expressionist tradition.

A VIEW OVER THE BOSPORUS. The Marangozhane Evi, literally 'the house of the carpenter's workshop', is so called because it was built as a workshop at the end of the nineteenth century by the leading carpenter in

The mixing of styles presents no problem to a painter interested above all in the interaction of form and colour. It is a game which Hale Arpacioğlu plays with subtlety and, on occasion, mischievousness. On this

pedestal table where one would expect a lamp she has placed a fine Kütahya pot, while above it hangs a late nineteenth-century canvas (left). Another example of the mixing of forms, this still life combines the opaline globe of an oil lamp with framed calligraphies and a gold-embroidered nineteenth-century silk scarf (above).

The strongest link between Hale Arpacioğlu's paintings and her flat is colour, and in particular red, a colour which abounds in her work.

In the sitting room (above), red features in the frames of two military decorations from the reign of Mehmet II on the mantelpiece, in one of her recent paintings, and in the carpet. In the attic room, a line of red chairs stands in front of one of her paintings, which dates from 1980. Hale Arpacioğlu sits next to a character from one of her paintings, her gaze fixed on a Manastir kilim from the late nineteenth century (left). Behind the Viennese settee, piled high with catalogues, is a fine 'Turkish primitive' landscape depicting Edirne (right).

The light of the Bosporus floods into the bedroom of Irem and Selçuk Erez. The room is decorated with Ottoman furniture and old kilims. The openwork blinds and the design of the windows are typical of traditional Turkish houses. Here the predominant white of the interior, which extends onto the balcony, gives a delightful airy atmosphere (above). All the magic and enchantment of Istanbul is encapsulated in this tea-time still life: an antique embroidered tablecloth, fruit, wisteria, chased silverware and traditional porcelain, including a fine Kütahya dish for the melon (right).

Turkey at that time, the Greek Andon Politis. It stands at the top of a hill overlooking the Bosporus, in the village of Boyacıköy on the European shore. When the interior designer Irem Erez and her husband Selçuk bought it a few years ago, this old Ottoman house was about to collapse. Its foundations were full of woodworm, its interior was dilapidated and the traditional features of its façade had disappeared. Irem Erez decided to have the façade restored and the interior totally rebuilt, so that the house might regain its former splendour.

The ghost of the Greek carpenter must be happy with his new home, which is now arranged on three levels, ingeniously incorporating a mezzanine and a study on a balcony bordered by a wooden banister. Light colours, together with Ottoman furniture, panelling and carpets have been carefully co-ordinated to create a deceptively simple effect.

It took Irem Erez six years to restore and furnish her house. The divans, wood panelling, banisters, calligraphies and embroidered silks recreate the Ottoman style of the

original house (left), which was built by Andon Politis, the carpenter responsible, amongst other things, for the woodwork in the Yıldız Palace.

MODERNITY WITHIN TRADITION

by Caroline Champenois

Y ou cannot be truly happy living in Istanbul without a love of its long history, its culture and its traditions. You constantly come across traces of Byzantium and Constantinople, insistent reminders of the city's rich past. To live in harmony with Istanbul you must understand and respect its history.

The homes of Istanbulites who love their city are invariably stamped, in one way or another, with the mark of tradition. Even when you visit a house or flat which is resolutely modern, you know at once that you are in Istanbul and nowhere else in the world. Such dwellings simply could never have been conceived in Paris, New York, or even Ankara.

The magic of Istanbul's long history can be felt everywhere: in the way a house opens onto the Bosporus, a reflection in a *tombak* dish, a Greek marble statue standing next to an Ottoman divan, the symmetry of a *yalı*, a floor paved in grey marble.

THE HOUSE OF LIGHTS. The village of Boyacıköy lies near Emirgan on the European shore of the Bosporus, and for a long time was mainly inhabited by Jews and Christians. Its narrow streets are lined with fine traditional houses, including a number of corbelled stone *konaks*. Ten years ago, Christine and Rony Grünberg fell in love with one such *konak* and bought it. It was one of four identical houses

built in 1920 to house professors from the university. The exterior boasted a listed traditional wooden façade. The interior of the house, however, posed a problem: it was made up of a plethora of tiny rooms, a design which was not at all in keeping with the Grünbergs' love of large spaces.

After much thought, they finally opted for the simplest solution: demolish the house, rebuild the exterior of the building exactly as it had been, then completely redesign the interior. They drew up a plan and entrusted its execution to some of Istanbul's best craftsmen. Then, when the shell of the house was completed, they asked the interior designer Rüya Nebioğlu, the owner of the famous Pink *yalı*, to design the inside of the house combining traditional and modern styles.

During the day natural light pours in through the skylight, while at night, the house is lit by a large mosque chandelier. The mezzanine floor is bordered by a moucharaby in Oregon pine, and is decorated with kilims and cushions made by Christine Grünberg using antique fabrics. A Tepfi brass tray serves as a low table displaying a collection of antique Turkish pipes (left). Directly beneath the light well, the small but splendid indoor garden, with its classical marble Ottoman fountain and its pebble mosaic, transforms the entrance hall into a patio (below).

Wood has been extensively used in the Grünbergs' house. The dining room features a fine Byzantine wood panel, which is in fact the headboard of a bed. The Thonet chairs were bought in a flea market in Istanbul (above). The woodwork in the drawing room (below right) has an air of mystery: the small carved niches decorating the wooden partition, retrieved from an eighteenth-century Anatolian house, are more numerous than is normal for this type of object. The wood goes well with the brass of the *mangal*, a traditional brazier which was used to heat people's houses, as does the coral-pink, early twentieth-century Bohemian tea service arranged on a clover-leaf pouffe.

The end result is one of the most attractive interiors in Istanbul. The various levels of the house are organized around a large light well, rather like a small *han* under a glass roof. The light floods into this well, beneath which grows a splendid indoor garden, arranged around a marble fountain and bordered by an intricate pebble mosaic.

The daylight filters from the well into the rest of the house through a modern version of a moucharaby, creating a dramatic chiaroscuro effect, as in a mosque, with light and shade playing on kilims, brass and antique panelling. At night the Grünbergs' delightful dinner parties are lit by the warm, golden glow of a mosque chandelier, in a charming dining room where guests, while enjoying their delicious and beautifully served meal, can feel almost as if they have been transported out of time.

Mosque chandeliers, like this one in the Grünbergs' dining room, often find their way into homes. They can be bought in the Covered Bazaar, but complete sets of antique glasses are becoming increasingly rare. Lighting them takes patience and dexterity: each glass receptacle is filled with water, a little olive oil is added then a small float, into which a wick is inserted, is placed on the oil. All that remains is to light the wicks, of which there are sometimes more than a dozen. They give off a soft and mysterious light (left).

The bedroom is filled with a pale light, filtered by Venetian blinds and the trees of the Istanbul University campus. This thoroughly modern interior has been created using antiques: a wooden chest which belonged to Lale Çavdar's grandmother; a *tombak* tray and candlestick; a lace bedspread; calligraphic panels; and the base of an antique column. The few modern elements—the large mirror and the contemporary Murano glassware—play only a secondary role in this metamorphosis (left). The three levels of this house, built in 1910 and entirely rebuilt by the Çavdars in 1980, are linked by cleverly positioned staircases, creating a cubist-like interior. A painting by the Turkish artist Birol Kutay is offset by the neutral colour of the walls (above).

In this corner of the sitting room, a large wooden bird—an African totem—keeps watch next to a Le Corbusier chaise longue. During the day the luxuriant vegetation of the garden and the minimalist interior create a striking contrast, one complementing the other like *yin* and *yang*. The granite paving slabs provide an agreeably cool surface in summer, whilst in winter, thanks to a system of underfloor heating, they radiate heat (above).

AN ARCHITECTS' HOUSE IN RUMELI HISARI. 'How can traditional Ottoman architecture be reconciled with the demands of modern design and comfort?' This must have been the question in the minds of Tuncan Çavdar and his son Aloş, both architects, when they bought a large traditional house surrounded by the trees of the Bosporus University campus at Rumeli Hisarı. They were immediately attracted to the house because, as they explained, 'it is located in one of those rare parts of the city where you feel as if you're both in the city and outside it'. But how do you live in a wooden house originally designed to accommodate an entire extended family, with 30 rooms with their original fittings,

all over a hundred years old? The answer is by rebuilding it from top to bottom, restoring its listed façade to its original condition, then furnishing and decorating it with a mixture of old and new, western and Ottoman, as has been the tradition in Istanbul for over a century.

For the Çavdars, who live here as a family, the contemporary takes precedence over, and transforms, the old. The bare walls emphasize the geometry of the traditional sash windows, making them seem modern; placing an old chest at the head of a bed in the middle of a bedroom becomes a wonderful innovation. The way in which the Çavdars have used concrete is the most spectacular example of their

creativity. Since they were obliged to preserve the traditional wooden façade of the house in its entirety, they had it meticulously reconstructed, but in a new material called 'concrete fibre', which looks like wood but has none of its drawbacks. Inside the house, the striking grey of the exposed concrete walls provides a neutral backdrop for the soft light and delicate colours, giving the interior an understated quality. Clearly the Çavdars have not allowed themselves to be overawed by Turkey's cultural heritage, but neither have they rejected it: like true artists they have tamed it, appropriating tradition and renewing it, creating a new style all of their own.

TWO HOUSES BY SEDAD ELDEM. Sedad Eldem, who died several years ago, is regarded as the greatest twentieth-century Turkish architect. Back in the 1930s he was the first Turkish architect to design buildings that were resolutely contemporary, but at the same time specifically Turkish. He paved the way for one of the main currents in contemporary Turkish architecture, which seeks to embrace the country's cultural heritage and shuns the uniformity of the International Style. Eldem's work brought him immediate acclaim, and in a career that spanned half a century he put his name to a multitude of major architectural projects. Two of his best-known buildings in Istanbul are the Faculty of

This Albini bookshelf, only partially filled so as to avoid creating a solid wall, serves as a partition in Tuncan Çavdar's spacious studio. The room also contains a Josef Hoffmann armchair and a large canvas by the Turkish painter Neset Gunal. A wooden floor seemed appropriate for the architects studio (above).

133

Rahmi Koç's beautiful collection of antiques and works of art is enhanced by the rigour of Sedad Eldem's architecture. His elegant office houses a collection of Greek, Roman and Hittite vases, along with antique globes, which doubtless evoke memories of his many trips abroad (right). The sky over the Bosporus is reflected in the windows of the house, which overlooks the Bay of Tarabya. The building's layout, the decorative motifs on the façade and even the design of the fireplaces recall, in stylized form, traditional Turkish architecture (below). The marble peristyle in the garden subtly echoes the rectangular forms of the house's façade. Suna Kıraç has added a fountain from a *hamam*, the sculpted motifs of which echo the neighbouring large-leaved plants (opposite page).

Science and Literature and the Law Courts.

But Sedad Eldem did not devote himself exclusively to prestigious monumental projects. As a devotee of the traditional architecture of the banks of the Bosporus, he designed a number of villas and *yalıs* which express, in a contemporary language, all the fine qualities of their ancestors.

The villa designed by Sedad Eldem for the industrialist Rahmi Koç on a plot of land overlooking the Bay of Tarabya, one of the most beautiful parts of the Bosporus, was completed in 1980. It is a perfect illustration of his concern with recreating the light and graceful style of traditional houses: the villa's façade consists of large windows and a glazed, cantilevered upper floor, while inside, a vast space, filled with light, contains a central *sofa* which extends out onto two terraces, one overlooking the Bosporus and the other the garden. Rahmi Koç is a keen art collector, and the interior is filled with treasures, including superb Chinese porcelain and magnificent carpets. Wood is the principal material inside the house. Particularly impressive is the immense wooden ceiling,

Suna Kıraç's *yalı*, designed by Sedad Eldem, encapsulates all the magic of the shores of the Bosporus: the horizontal and vertical lines of the building echo and reinforce the verticals of the trees and minarets and the horizontals of the river. The main hall on the ground floor contains some of the finest pieces from Suna Kıraç's various collections. Beneath the stairs, a sixteenth-century Edirne settee decorated with carved, gilt motifs is framed by two large sixteenth-century *tombak* candleholders (below).

which is in the form of the base of a pyramid.

In 1965, at Vaniköy on the opposite shore of the Bosporus, Sedad Eldem designed a two-storey *yalı* for Suna Kıraç, Rahmi Koç's sister. Here the simplicity and rigorous symmetry of the traditional *yalı* has been respected and even highlighted: the façade is made up of glazed rectangles, while inside, the bedrooms frame a central *sofa*. Yalıs are essentially summer residences which are unoccupied for a large part of the year. But Sedad Eldem did not want this one to become just another lifeless empty property in winter. Its strong geometric and sculptural qualities ensure that the building is pleasing to the eye all year round. In winter the façade, with its closed wooden shutters framed in white, neatly matches the rectangular pattern on the ground created by the dark paving stones edged in lighter marble. In summer, when the shutters are open, the light of the Bosporus streams through the 40 windows, illuminating the refined decor, which, just as Suna Kıraç had wanted, reproduces the atmospheric style of a traditional Ottoman interior.

This sitting room opens out onto the main hall. The geometric sobriety of Sedad Eldem's architecture provides a neutral setting for the bright colours of the carpets, fabrics and old paintings. Above an Ottoman divan hangs a portrait by Georg Engelhardt

Schröder (1684-1750) of Mehmet Saït Celebi, ambassador of the Sublime Porte. Next to him stands another important figure in Ottoman history, Ibrahim Muteferica, who introduced printing with Arabic characters into the empire (left). Suna Kıraç owns a magnificent collection of *tombak* artefacts, including this eighteenth-century ewer (above).

A DUPLEX BY THE SEA OF MARMARA. For many years, the fine *yalı* belonging to the Verdi family sat peacefully in the elegant village of Suadiye, about ten kilometres south of Üsküdar by the Sea of Marmara. Gradually, however, the village was swallowed up by the city, and the building of a new coast road meant that the *yalı*

Bare walls, an ornate eighteenth-century Anatolian door, a piece of seventeenth-century velvet with gold-embroidered tulip motifs and eighteenth-century Edirne chairs create an interior of subtle contrasts.

had to be demolished. The Verdis got permission to construct a block of flats on the same land, next to the new road, and they decided that they would include include a spacious duplex flat for themselves. They wanted the new flat to keep the memory of their *yalı* alive, by preserving something of the latter's lost splendour. Anyone less inspired would probably have been tempted to build some kind of replica or pastiche, but the Verdis, with the help of architects Havan Mingu and Mehmet Konuralp, had the good sense not to let nostalgia determine the aspect of the building. Ferhunde Verdi, who designed the interior of the new home, thought that the best way of remaining true to the spirit of the old *yalı* would be to design a contemporary interior that reflected its own time. In her view, there were really only two elements of the original *yalı* that could be transposed successfully into the present: the sense of space, and the marvellous combination of simplicity and refinement common to all *yalıs*.

Ferhunde Verdi has applied these principles lavishly: the traditional large spaces have become immense—the living room, for example, covers an area of more than 250 square metres. Simplicity has become purity; in the smooth walls painted in pale ochre, in the omnipresent right angles, and in the geometric white surround of the fireplace. As for the element of refinement, it has become sumptuous good taste: only furniture and decorative features that are beautiful, precious and antique have been selected.

Every object has been carefully displayed in an elaborate interplay of colours and volumes. The Verdi's lost *yalı* has been reborn in a strikingly contemporary style . . .

Two staircases side by side: the one leading to the upper floor of the duplex and the other formed by the lines of calligraphy on a seventeenth-century *firman* (decree), which seems to ascend towards the fine *tuğra* (monogram) of Sultan Mehmet IV (above).

In one corner of the main living room, the bar counter is the only contemporary element which is not vertical. It is entirely covered in gold leaf and its recess contains a collection of Persian and Ottoman artefacts from the twelfth and thirteenth centuries. The small statue is Roman and the bas-relief frieze, cut in half so that it can be viewed in its entirety, is Hellenistic (right).

The house designed by Mehmet Konuralp for Ayşegül and Tayfun Uzunova (right) is a contemporary but nonetheless graceful version of the traditional symmetrical design of Ottoman residences, a symmetry reaccentuated by the building's reflection in the water of the swimming pool (below). Ayşegül Uzunova, who has worked in fashion for 20 years and frequently travels in her job, came across this 1930s leather settee in a Paris flea market and it now stands in her husband's study. It was her husband, on the other hand, who acquired the large portrait by the Turkish painter Komet, because of its resemblance to Ayşegül. A Tizio lamp and some boxes brought back from India have been arranged on a Thonet pedestal table (right).

AT ÇENGELKÖY, BETWEEN SKY AND WATER. When a woman who enjoys picking up beautiful things in the course of her travels decorates a house designed by a highly talented architect the result is bound to be remarkable.

This is the case with the house of Ayşegül and Tayfun Uzunova, situated on the hill at Çengelköy. It was built in 1986 and designed by the architect Mehmet Konuralp. Here again the architect has adhered to a traditional symmetrical layout, but the two wings with their cut-away sides, the cantilevered upper storey and the overhanging roof give this house a distinctly original and contemporary flavour.

The charming interior was improvised by Ayşegül Uzunova around various objects gleaned from antique shops, chiefly in France and Italy. The meeting of sky with water creates a magical combination of fluidity, reflections, light and transparency. The eclectic collection of antiques and furniture is perfectly complemented by certain elements used in the decoration of the interior: mirrors are artfully positioned to reflect objects; glass tables are

A feminine touch can be found in Ayşegül Uzunova's bedroom—a wicker chair bought in Paris is reflected in an Ecole de Nancy art nouveau dressing table (below). In summer the Uzunovas like to entertain on the terrace by the pool. The table is covered with a piece of embroidered Ottoman fabric. The hilltop location offers a number of delights, such as the fresh air, the light and the famous

Çengelköy gherkins, which, in Ayşegül's opinion, are the best in the world (above). Opening out onto the terrace, its polished granite floor reflecting the sky, the dining room feels almost as if it were outdoors. The round table, designed by Norman Foster, is surrounded by contemporary Thonet dining chairs. The delicate art deco console table was bought in Milan. On it stand two fine *alems* made out of *tombak*. These symbolic sculptures used to decorate the domes of mosques and can occasionally be found in good antique shops in Istanbul (below right and opposite page).

used so as not to obscure them; and the perfect reflections of trees and sky on the polished granite floor make them seem as if they are floating in space. The granite floor is edged with marble inlay in a checker pattern, like a magic carpet as transparent as a veil.

The sky is present in the house even where it cannot actually be seen: the windows in the rooms on the first floor are topped with squares of blue glass, which transform the shadow of the overhanging roof into a summer sky.

As for water, the swimming pool acts like a giant mirror reflecting the house. In order to avoid the 'swimming pool blue' which she detests, Ayşegül Uzunova had the pool lined with anthracite grey fibreglass. This heightens the pool's reflective quality: it is as if a silvering had been applied to the water, creating a magic mirror capable of transforming day into

night. The reflection of the house in the deep blue water creates yet another symmetry, vertical and like the night sky, while the ochre façade, inspired by the owner's love of Italy, glows like moonlight.

PALACES OF THE BOSPORUS

by Gérard-Georges Lemaire

The flamboyant pavilions and kiosks
of Topkapı Palace, resembling some encampment
of nomadic lords suddenly fixed in stone,
or nineteenth-century waterside palaces, mingling every
conceivable influence from East and West—these
were the creations of one of the most sumptuous
empires in history. Today they bear witness to
the splendours of the past.

Shortly after he captured Constantinople in 1453, Sultan Mehmet II ordered that a new palace be built to celebrate the triumph of the Osman dynasty. It took some 15 years to complete and he named it the House of Happiness. In time, however, it came to be known as Topkapı Sarayı, literally the Cannon Gate Palace. There is nothing overstated, nothing monumental or pompous about this nerve centre of an empire which, by then, spanned three continents. In fact, it looks more like some kind of huge encampment. When the French poet and politician Alphonse de Lamartine visited it in 1833, he commented on its striking layout: 'The courtyards and gardens, formed by the empty spaces between the kiosks, are irregularly arranged and irregularly planted.' The buildings, arranged around three courtyards which follow each other in a symbolic order, give the impression of being tents built out of stone and marble. The awnings which decorate some of the buildings and the majestic gates reinforce this effect, creating the disturbing illusion of a nomadic architecture suddenly fixed in time.

Over the centuries, successive sultans enlarged the complex and added their own embellishments, each leaving his mark by building new pavilions or adding new pieces to this unusual puzzle. At the end of the seventeenth century, the shifting of the harem closer to the sultan's apartments further reinforced the labyrinthine quality of the palace, a quality which immediately strikes anyone who ventures into it.

Lamartine was struck by the palace's furnishings, which mixed magnificence with extreme simplicity: 'The doors to the imperial chambers were open; we saw a large number of rooms, all of which were similar both in layout and in the decoration of their gilded, moulded ceilings. Cupolas of wood and marble, pierced with arabesque apertures . . .; low, wide divans lining the walls; no furniture, no chairs, only carpets, mats and cushions; windows which begin six inches from the floor and look out over courtyards, galleries, terraces and gardens; that is everything.'

At the time of Lamartine's visit to Topkapı Palace, the old seraglio had already been abandoned by the Sultan Mahmut II, who had chosen to live in a large imperial summer residence built of wood, which was located at Beşiktaş near the Bosporus. In Ohsson's *Tableau général de l'Empire ottoman* there is a wonderful engraving which gives us some idea of the enchanting beauty of the spot. This palace, so dear to Mahmut II, was demolished by his successor Abdül Mecit and replaced by the Dolmabahçe Palace. Built between 1842 and 1853, and designed by Karabet Balyan and his son Nikoğos, it was to be the first of the *sahil sarayı* (water palaces) which grace the

When Alphonse de Lamartine made his second trip to Constantinople in 1850, he discovered palaces which had not been built when he first visited the capital of the Ottoman Empire. He was stupefied by the 'water palaces': 'Our oriental palaces can give no idea of these semi-Indian structures, which are both gigantic and fantastic like the imagination of Orientals . . . Small marble columns, vaults filled with winding arabesques, terraces with lattices, stained-glass windows, balustrades with flowers; balconies jutting from every storey, their windows open to the breathing of the waves; porticoes for as far as you can see, opening out on one side onto the sea, and on the other onto avenues of cypresses . . .'
The façade of Beylerbeyi Palace (preceding double page).
The country pavilion at Ilhamur. It was here that Lamartine met the young Sultan Abdül Mecit (opposite page). A gateway at Dolmabahçe Palace (above).

The novelist Edmondo de Amicis, like Lamartine, was dazzled by the strange imperial lounges, nearly all of which were designed by the Balyan family. Dolmabahçe fascinated him. He described it as a breathtaking synthesis of all the styles in the world: 'One sees mixed together in a confusion which one has never seen elsewhere Arabic, Greek, Turkish, Romanesque and Renaissance styles. There is an indescribable profusion of ornaments, thrown together, as a Turkish poet puts it, by the hand of a madman . . . It appears that it couldn't have been a peaceful Armenian architect who had the first idea, but rather a sultan in love who saw it in a dream whilst sleeping in the arms of his most ambitious lover.'
The conservatory at Dolmabahçe (opposite page) and one of the fountains which adorn the garden (below).

shores of the Bosporus. Théophile Gautier, who witnessed the palace being built in the summer of 1852, described it rapturously: 'This vast construction in Marmara marble, of a bluish white which appears slightly cold on account of its newness, produces a powerfully majestic effect between the blue of the sky and the blue of the sea . . .' While he is plainly amazed at the hybrid nature of the façade with its neo-classical Renaissance design, he grants that 'one cannot deny that this profusion of flowers, foliage, ceiling roses carved like jewels in precious stone, has an intricate, complex and sumptuous aspect which is pleasing to the eye.'

Gautier was able to visit the building in the company of its architect, and he was surprised at being able to enter the sultan's apartments, which were 'in an orientalized Louis XIV style, where one senses an intention to imitate the splendours of Versailles: the doors, the windows and their frames are of cedar, mahogany and rosewood, intricately carved, and are fitted with splendid hinges covered with gold leaf.' This combination of eastern and western tastes was to be an abiding feature of the palaces of the Bosporus.

The imperial residence at Küçüksu (1856-1857) designed by Nikoğos Balyan, the Çirağan Palace at Beşiktaş (1874) and the Beylerbeyi Palace (1865), both designed by Sarkis Balyan, have similar characteristics and the same style of decor. They are united by their excess, their extravagance, their ostentatious luxury, and a strange poetry created by the extraordinary contradictions and juxtapositions of irreconcilable periods and styles. The huge Bohemian crystal candelabra, the heavy chandeliers dripping with Baccarat crystal, the

furniture which belongs neither to East nor West but to a dream carried to excess—all this provided the dramatic setting within which the compelling drama of the end of an empire was played out.

The final act, however, took place at Yıldız. Abdül Hamit, who became known as the Red Sultan, decided to leave Dolmabahçe and take up residence in the curious şale, or chalet, tucked away in the wooded section of the park. He spent lavish sums on creating the gardens, aided by an army of architects, landscape artists and gardeners, and in order to embellish this enchanting retreat, completely shut off from the world, he filled it with pavilions, small ornamental lakes, rambling paths, fanciful bridges, a small theatre with a blue cupola (where, it is said, Sarah Bernhardt once performed), a sumptuous mosque and the Küçük Mabeyn, a lavish reception building designed in the French style.

In the late summer of 1922, the green and gold imperial caïque, rowed by 14 oarsmen, drew alongside the quay at Dolmabahçe. The last sultan, Mehmet VI, was about to leave his Yıldız retreat. He boarded the magnificent craft and was conveyed to the destroyer which was to take him far from the Sublime Porte, far from an empire which no longer existed. Atatürk turned Topkapı and most of the palaces on the coast of the Bosporus into national museums.

A glorious page in the long history of Turkey had been turned. It had begun with Osman Gazi at the beginning of the fourteenth century, and definitively ended in 1924 with the departure into exile of the heir apparent, Abdül Mecit, who went to France to live as an artist.

In 1852 Théophile Gautier had the good fortune to visit Dolmabahçe in the company of its architect, Nikoǧos Balyan. He was astonished at the sight of a huge room that was 'capped by a dome of red glass. When the sun shone through this ruby dome, everything inside seemed to blaze with fire. The air itself seemed to ignite, and it was as if you were breathing fire; the columns lit up like street lamps.' Corinthian columns and monumental staircases with Baccarat crystal banisters (left and above) lead to the extraordinary throne room. In this palace even the fireplaces and chairs are made of Baccarat crystal (below).

The author of the *Roman de la momie* did not find at Dolmabahçe the oriental splendours of which he was so fond. Rather he found rooms decorated 'in an orientalized Louis XIV style. . . . In one of the rooms of this palace will be installed the Louis XIV salon, which was built and decorated in Paris by Séchan, the distinguished decorator of the Opéra.' Théophile Gautier observes that the sultan could have drawn on the decorative resources of the East, but 'in line with the kind of fancy that leads us to build Alhambras in Paris . . .', he 'wanted a palace to accord with modern taste'. One of the Louis XIV-style drawing rooms in the imperial apartments (left), and the Salon of the Ambassadors (below).

The first imperial palace at Yıldız was built for Selim III's mother in the early nineteenth century. With the accession of Abdül Hamit II in 1876, it was to become the administrative centre of the empire. He had a wooden palace built, together with pavilions scattered around the park, an ornamental lake, ponds, bridges, a large glasshouse, a mosque and a reception building. The Şale Pavilion, the principal residence, is relatively modest, discounting the large Reception Hall and the monumental staircase (preceding pages), and it gives a paradoxical image of Ottoman power in decline. The decor of the drawing rooms is an extreme expression of the tension between the Moorish and the French rococo styles (above, left and right).

The nineteenth-century Ottoman aesthetic is summed up in the residences that lie along the banks of the Bosporus. Claude Farrère describes them well: 'For a distance of 20 kilometres from Constantinople, the banks are completely covered with exquisite *yalıs*—that is to say summer residences.' Referring to the palaces, Farrère says: 'Imagine small versions of Versailles, or small Trianons . . .' The sultan's apartments on the first floor of the Beylerbeyi Palace have typical eighteenth-century European furniture, together with Moorish tables (far left, left and below). The oculi, English-style bow windows, Turkish curtains and oriental carpets of this particular room create a strange atmosphere.

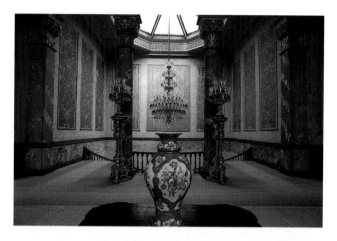

The Beylerbeyi Palace, the summer residence of Abdül Aziz, was completed in 1865. Some 25 years later, Pierre Loti had occasion to arrive at its quayside 'of spotless white marble, in front of deserted palaces, with white and gold railings. Within these uninhabited palaces there are . . . a forest of columns of every colour, a jumble of lamps and candelabra, intricately decorated ceilings in the oriental style, and Bursa silks and brocades.' The monumental staircase which leads to the Blue Room is the epitome of this make-believe baroque that was cultivated by the sultans of the reform era. The columns made of imitation blue marble encircled with gold, the gigantic Bohemian crystal candelabra, the huge chandelier inlaid with blue and gold and the Moorish capitals are the expression of an art in search of an identity, torn between the East of tradition and the West of progress (right and above).

When Edmondo de Amicis visited
Topkapı Palace, he attempted to
reconstruct for his reader the intricate
geography of this inextricable citadel.
He describes the buildings as 'scattered
here and there' in the midst of groves
and gardens. 'These were the baths of
Selim II, all marble, gold and paintings;
kiosks, both octagonal and round,
topped by cupolas and roofs of every
shape which capped smaller rooms,

inlaid with mother-of-pearl and
decorated with Arabic inscriptions, and
where, in every window, hung gilded
cages containing nightingales and
parakeets. . . . To some of these kiosks
the *padischahs* would come to have
the *Thousand and One Nights* read to
them by ageing dervishes . . .'
The roofs, pinnacles, cupolas, towers
and turrets of Topkapı create an
impression of fantastical anarchy, yet
they do follow a labyrinthine pattern
(preceding double page).
Topkapı's ceramic tiles feature floral
motifs which combine abstract
patterns with meticulous realism
(opposite page, left and above).

At Topkapı at the beginning of the eighteenth century, the harem was installed next to the sultan's apartments. In 1720, during the reign of Ahmet III, Lady Montagu, wife of the English ambassador at the sultan's court, had an opportunity to visit it and was astonished by the elegance and splendour of this enigmatic labyrinth. The Royal Salon in the harem (left) had none of the simplicity of the apartments in the old seraglio. Opulence, ostentation and grandiloquence predominate in a mixture of styles. The painted panels in the Fruit Room give a sense of the hedonistic elegance which reigned in the microcosm of the harem (above).

TRADITIONS

by Teresa Battesti

The geometric patterns of kilims and
the shimmering colours of carpets; flowers
painted on walls or embroidered on silk;
gleaming brasswork reflecting the light of the
Bosporus; the sacred art of calligraphy:
Istanbul's traditional crafts continue
to flourish in all their extraordinary
complexity and beauty.

In Istanbul traditional crafts reflect a diverse and constantly evolving culture, yet are the product of techniques which have remained essentially unchanged for centuries. The creative genius of Istanbul's craftsmen lies in their ability to tailor the heritage of the past to the changing needs of the present. Ever since the Iron Age, Turkish crafts have been continually enriched by influences from central Asia, Europe, and, above all, Islam. An all-embracing religion, Islam regulates the lives of Muslims and is expressed in, and embodied by, the objects of day-to-day life. Most of the crafts are represented in the *hamams*, which have been such an essential part of life in Istanbul. The traditional crafts consist principally of carpet-weaving, ceramics, gold plate and jewellery, metalwork, calligraphy and embroidery. The decorative motifs are inspired by the largely abstract and symbolic forms of Islamic art. There are four basic decorative elements in Islamic art; geometric figures, floral motifs, calligraphy, and animal and human representations. However, while this decorative language confines the craftsman within the rules of an overall unity, it does not mean that he lacks freedom of expression.

CARPETS. Carpets are an inextricable feature of Turkish life. As the proverb says: 'Where your carpet is, that is your home.' In earlier times, carpets were essential elements in the lives of Anatolian nomads. Decorated with simple abstract and geometric motifs, they were either laid on the ground or doubled as tent canvases. Gradually they were incorporated into the interiors of Ottoman houses, palaces and mosques, in the form of court carpets and prayer mats, and their colours became brighter and patterns more varied.

'Each one has its own decorative language. Each one is a woven and patterned poem. Some have all the lushness of a meadow, while others are as dry as the desert sands. One by one, before your eyes, they unfold their language and enigma. Some are eloquent, others are mysterious. Carpets of conquerors, carpets of wise men, carpets of sombre reverie, carpets of exaltation, carpets of ecstasy. We flick through them one by one with our eyes. One suggests a butterfly's wing, another the mosaic of a stained-glass window. Some seem to be sleeping, while others are strangely alive, eluding us or signalling to us.' This variety, so vividly described by Henri de Régnier in *Escales en Méditerranée* (1931), is one of the

The decoration on this gilt wooden throne in the admirably restored Beylerbeyi Palace reflects the enthusiasm for baroque decoration and architecture which characterizes Istanbul's nineteenth-century royal palaces . The shop owned by leading carpet expert Şişko Osman in the Zincirli Han near the Covered Bazaar conceals a wealth of treasures. His older kilims are protected from the light and dust by white sheets embroidered with gold and silver thread. Each kilim has a distinctive pattern, characteristic of the particular tribe in Thrace or Anatolia that produced it, and the motifs are based on symbols that go back over thousands of years (right). Ceiling bosses such as these (opposite page), which date from the eighteenth and nineteenth centuries and are made of walnut, oak and mahogany, can be found in the antique shop owned by Yaman Mursaloğlu. Wood was widely used as an ornamental feature in Ottoman architecture, seen in carved ceilings, columns, door panels and banisters.

172

The kilim storeroom of the Adnan shop in the Covered Bazaar (above). Kilims are stored in the traditional way, by size and provenance. On the ground floor, kilims and knotted carpets are unrolled one by one for the benefit of customers. Each element of their design reflects the history of this art whose origins are lost in the mists of time (right). Şişko Osman wanted the decor of his shop to reflect the variety of his carpets, so the interior evokes both the simplicity of nomad tents and the splendour of an Ottoman palace. Kilims cover the walls and carpets are stacked on the floor: the two different worlds finally come together (opposite page).

most outstanding features of Turkish carpets.

Halıs are thick, soft carpets made with knotted stitches of wool, silk or cotton. They feature a wide variety of motifs, representing, with great delicacy and sometimes even realism,

anything from a garden full of flowers to a tree with birds on its branches or the hunting of wild animals on a plain. Striking arabesques, intricate geometrical patterns and interlaced miniature motifs create a complex tableau which invites the eye to linger. Kilims are usually woven using wool or a mix of wool and cotton. On rare occasions, silk is used. They are flat and slightly rough to the touch, generally with simple, geometric motifs characteristic of the particular region of Thrace or Anatolia in which they were woven. They are spread on the floor, hung on walls, or sewn into cushions and bags. Their decorative quality lies in their very simplicity, the skilful marriage of colours and

By the sixteenth century the Seljuks already had a well-organized system of guilds for silk-weavers. The numerous caravanserais built along the Silk Road at this time testify to the scale of the silk trade between East and West. Here at the Halılı Han, the Carpet Han, situated on the outskirts of Istanbul, the subtly coloured skeins of Anatolian silk, being used to make a carpet, glitter in the sunlight (left). The carpets made here are sold in the Covered Bazaar. Techniques have altered over the years, but the artistry remains unchanged: with hanks of silk hanging close at hand, a woman works on a knotted silk carpet. Using a loom makes it possible to produce longer carpets. Here silk is being used for the pile, but the warp and weft can be of cotton. As for the knot, these days it is generally tied across four threads of warp (above and below).

Şişko Osman's carpet shop opens onto a courtyard in the Zincirli Han, which dates from the seventeenth century (above and right). This is one of Istanbul's most secret shops, open only by arrangement. It operates from an outbuilding of the Rüstem Paşa Mosque, designed by Sinan and built in about 1550 (opposite page). The carved wooden ceiling, the arches, the calligraphy and the Iznik tiles provide a sumptuous backdrop for fine silks and carpets. A piece of yellow antique Bokhara fabric decorated with *suzani* chain-stitch embroidery can be seen in the foreground.

pureness of line which ensures they look good anywhere.

Istanbul is a city of carpets. You see them in the bazaars, in people's houses, in palaces and mosques, and of course in the museums, where some of the finest examples are exhibited. In the Kilim Museum in the Blue Mosque there is a collection of exceptionally fine kilims from various regions of Thrace and Anatolia. They provide a fascinating insight into this weaving tradition, in which Kurds, nomadic Turkomans and Seljuk Turks have vied with each other. This continually evolving tradition is still alive today, successfully adapting its designs in line with the requirements of an

increasingly discerning and appreciative western clientele. Not far from the Kilim Museum, in a group of former warehouses adjoining the Blue Mosque, there is the Carpet Museum. Here one can admire the splendour and crafts-

manship of *halıs* from Kayseri, Sivas, Konya, Bergama and Antalya. Elsewhere, the Museum of Turkish and Islamic Arts, housed in the Ibrahim Paşa Palace, exhibits the oldest known kilims. They date from the thirteenth century, the time of Marco Polo, who wrote in 1283 that the finest carpets in the world were woven at Konya, which at that time was the capital of the Seljuk dynasty.

The first prayer mats—the point at which simple woven cloths evolved into works of art—were woven in Anatolia in the fifteenth century. They are pure expressions of individual and collective faith, and bear a motif representing the *mihrab*, the niche inside mosques which indicates the direction of Mecca. The form and pattern of the *mihrab* varies. Ghiordes mats, for example, are noted for their dotted-line *mihrab*, those from Kula have a *mihrab* which is elaborately decorative, while mats from Ladik feature a *mihrab* with small columns.

The finest carpets, of course, were made for the salons and mosques of the palaces in workshops that were set up by the sultans. The court carpets which originated in the sultans' workshop at Uşak in western Anatolia were enormously fashionable, both in Turkey and in Europe, from the sixteenth century onwards. They often feature in the backgrounds of paintings by European artists, and in particular Holbein—to such an extent that they are sometimes called 'Holbein carpets'. They were made using the Ghiordes or 'symmetrical' knot, which is tied across two threads of warp, but sometimes, to give a carpet a more velvety appearance and finer detail, the Persian knot was used, tied on a single thread of warp.

All the splendour of the Ottoman Empire is

visible in the magnificent Uşak carpets, which were the first to introduce the medallion motif into Turkish art and which often feature the four flowers that were emblematic first of the seraglio and later of the entire country: the carnation, the hyacinth, the tulip and the rose.

Ceramics have flourished in Istanbul for centuries, with beautiful tiles adorning palaces, mosques, and, nowadays, the homes of connoisseurs. In the Gorbon factory, the tiles are baked in refractory moulds at low temperatures in order to prevent the colours from running (opposite page). Iznik tiles are renowned for their quality, the finesse of their designs and their intense, vibrant colours. These fine examples, decorated with cypress and flower motifs, date from the sixteenth century and feature the famous 'Iznik red', which was developed, after a long period of trial and error, using a combination of iron oxide and quartz (left). In the painting studio at the Gorbon tile factory traditional motifs are reproduced in painstaking detail (below).

This *han* next to the
Nuruosmaniye Mosque and
not far from the Covered Bazaar
is a quarter unto itself, with its
haphazard arrangement of
dwellings, its small shops and
craft workshops (right).
All of these bustling *hans* have
delightful corners where the
past suddenly leaps out at you,
as in this door of a caravanserai
that seems to open onto a
dream (above). In the
Galatasaray quarter, where
many cabinet-makers work, an
armchair heroically endures
having its joints clamped (left).

Not far from the Süleymaniye, an entire quarter, Dökmeciler, is given over to foundries. Here every kind of object is made, from the precious to the everyday. The bronze, copper and brass founders (*dökmeci*) are the inheritors of a tradition which extends back over 3,500 years and reached its peak during the Seljuk dynasty. The Dökmeciler foundries produce high-quality castings for such things as decorative fittings, cups, ashtrays, braziers, hookah-covers, taps and doorknobs (above and below). In this workshop the moulds are being prepared. In earlier days, the molten metal was poured into stone moulds, but nowadays a mould made of a sand amalgam, held within two frames of either iron or aluminium, is used (right).

Several Istanbul *hans* house the workshops of gold- and silversmiths (right and below). Jewellery and precious plate are produced using techniques that have been refined over hundreds of years. Today's products are a match for any of the gold and silver artefacts that were so prized by the Ottoman aristocracy. The Topkapı Palace maintained its own gold- and silversmiths to produce gold and silver plate and jewellery for the sultan and his retinue. Two sultans were themselves goldsmiths, because custom demanded that the sovereign practise a manual trade of some kind. In a chiaroscuro corner of a goldsmith's workshop, scales, shears, moulds, lathes, shavings of silver and, of course, a safe, sit side by side in that studied chaos which is one of the delights of Istanbul (right).

The interplay of contrasting colours imparts an impression of three-dimensional space to these enormous carpets on which courtiers used to grovel during audiences with the sultan. The mere sight of them conjures up visions of an opulent salon in some palace.

In 1843 Sultan Abdül Mecit set up the Hereke workshop, 70 kilometres east of Istanbul on the Gulf of Izmit. This workshop, which previously produced silk for the ladies of the seraglio, is still operational. The town has given its name to a characteristic local carpet made of silk and wool using the Ghiordes knot technique. They have light-coloured backgrounds and a wide variety of motifs, which vary according to fashion, ranging from classic Persian designs to art nouveau. Sultan Abdül Hamit had a large number of these carpets made for his palace at Yıldız Palace, including the enormous and exceptionally beautiful one in the great hall.

CERAMICS. The shimmering designs that appear on carpets can also be found on the ceramic tiles which adorn the walls and columns of mosques and palaces. Between the sixteenth and eighteenth centuries, the golden age of Turkish ceramic art, the most beautiful buildings were hung with veritable tapestries

of ceramic tiles. It was during the sixteenth century that production at Iznik reached its peak. Until the time when production ceased at the beginning of the eighteenth century, Iznik tiles, with their glazed polychrome floral designs, set the style for Turkish ceramics. Executed with extraordinary finesse, the tiles glinted and shone in shadowy interiors. The rainbow range of their seven colours metamorphosed into the colours of a spring garden: turquoise, deep blue, black, purple, white, pistachio-green and yellow. These last two were quickly replaced by leaf-green and the famous tomato-red, the introduction of which in the middle of the sixteenth century marked the high point of Ottoman ceramics. Süleyman's great architect Sinan utilized this

Calligraphy is a sacred art and nowhere in the world does it inspire such fervour as in Turkey. In the calm atmosphere of the former *medrese*, or school of Islamic law, in the Süleymaniye mosque complex, precious antique Korans are painstakingly restored (opposite page). The workshop opens onto the garden via a superb arched window in the shape of a *mihrab*.

Aysegül Nadir owns an impressive collection of artefacts all of which represent the conjunction of art and religion: illuminated manuscripts, calligraphies proclaiming the name of Allah, a text laid out in the form of a dervish's hat, jaspar and carnelian rosary beads and quill pens (below). Dating from the fourteenth century, this Koran belonged to Sultan Beyazıt. It is in the process of being restored in the specialist workshop at the Süleymaniye (opposite page).

symphony of colours when, in around 1560, he dressed the architectural forms of the mosque of Rüstem Paşa in a scintillating, multi-patterned coat of tiles. The kilns at Kütahya, which took over from Iznik, still produce tiles which are inspired by that golden age.

The designs on Iznik pottery were as refined as those of the tiles. Lotuses and billowing clouds mingled with floral compositions on plates that might also be edged with chinoiserie in the shape of waves and rocks. Jugs were decorated with flowery foliage, goblets covered in serrated leaves and the bulbous necks of bottles stamped with medallions. The Museum of Ceramics in the Çinili Köşkü (the Tiled Pavilion) at Topkapı houses several of these pieces, so lavishly executed that one forgets that they are made of the humblest of materials: clay.

The ceramics of Çanakkale, on the Asian shore of the Dardanelles, appeared at the end of the eighteenth century. The Sadberk Hanım Museum, in a handsome restored *yalı* at Büyükdere by the Bosporus, has a fine collection of Çanakkale pottery, featuring plates decorated with slightly naïve geometric and floral motifs and zoomorphic pot-bellied jugs with spiral handles. The museum also has a collection of porcelain from the Yıldız workshop established by Abdül Hamit II to supply the palace with imitation Sèvres and Dresden china. It was reopened in 1962 and is still operating today.

Far from being dead, the ceramic tradition is flourishing. The inventiveness of talented ceramists such as Fürreya Koral and Alev Siesbiye, whose work is exhibited in museums all around the world, have given this art form a new lease of life.

This muslin stole, with its foliage, garlands and bouquets embroidered in gold thread, dates from the early nineteenth century. It is trimmed with an *oya* border made of gold thread needle-lace. This exquisite piece of work can be seen at the embroidery school at the Olgunlasma Institute (left). At the embroidery school, this piece of velvet (above) is being embroidered with laminated gold thread and is held at the required height by a wooden clamp. The embroidery frames used by the ladies of the seraglio, with their mother-of-pearl inlays and precious marquetries, have disappeared, but the methods are virtually unchanged. The fabric is held in a frame, and threads of silver, gold and silk are embroidered onto it following a pattern marked out beforehand (below).

Exquisite lace and embroidery combined with the light, sensual quality of silk: part of a nineteenth-century ceremonial oufit (right). Traditionally a young woman was not permitted to speak in front of her mother-in-law, and was expected to mind what she said before her husband. Embroidery became her language—through flowers and patterns she was able to express her feelings. In a shop in the Covered Bazaar a secret world of women is embodied in these bath towels and gauze scarves embroidered with gold thread. They have been placed in a velvet box decorated with silver, which dates from the nineteenth century. Such boxes were traditionally part of a bride's trousseau (below).

METALWORK. Istanbul's collectors have a predilection, shared by connoisseurs all over the world, for Seljuk metalwork, which originated on the banks of the Amu Darya between Persia and China, and then flourished on the ruins of ancient Byzantium. From the Chinese and Persians it took the techniques of engraving, *repoussé*, gilding and inlaying with niello, and from Byzantium it took the art of *cloisonné* enamel. This synthesis led to the development of ingenious alloys of copper, bronze and brass to imitate the textures of gold and silver, although the Koran prohibited the use of items made from them for domestic purposes. A tradition of casting metal also developed, producing items such as braziers, mortars, incense-burners, mirrors, candlesticks, drums and banner-holders. Their forms were inspired by animals and architecture.

Other techniques were also developed, including polychrome inlays which led to a flowering of figurative composition dominated by pictures of sultans, hunting scenes and mythological creatures. Vermeil was reserved for the most precious objects, so for normal

Five traditional textiles expressing all the refinement and splendour of a civilization: gold embroidery on the mauve velvet of a bridal dress which is called a *bindallı*—literally 'a thousand branches'; a dark red bedspread decorated with a bouquet of flowers

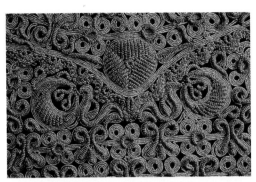

and ears of corn; gold roses along the edge of a towel; silver braiding on the jacket of an embassy guard; flowering carnations on a silk scarf. They were all made in the nineteenth century, with the exception of the silk scarf, which dates from the sixteenth century (left and above).

This small chased dish of tin-plated copper contains henna powder (below), which is obtained by grinding the dried leaves and bark of the henna bush, and is used by women to dye their hair, hands and feet. The 'henna night' is still very much alive as a tradition: on the night before her wedding, a bride's hands and feet are dyed by women from the family of her future husband.

Palaces of marble and water designed for the twin purposes of purification and relaxation, *hamams* are an essential part of life in Istanbul. The *hamam* at Cağaloğlu was built in the eighteenth century (opposite page). The steam-room combines simplicity and refinement: the decoration on the fountains and the chased copper taps is offset by the sobre columns and the heated marble slabs on which bathers stretch out to sweat and be massaged.

use goldsmiths would often employ an alloy of copper and zinc whose colour was reminiscent of gold. *Tombak*, the technique of gilding copper with mercury, was used for everything from the shields and helmets of Janissaries to the perfume-burners used in the harems, and became a part of everyday life in the palaces of the Ottoman aristocracy.

Nowadays in Istanbul you find copper on every street corner, in the form of *alems* (the ornaments on the tops of mosques), self-righting trays designed so as not to spill the coffee, coffee-sets, locks and padlocks, and the boxes used by shoeshine boys. Most of these items are produced in tiny metalwork shops close to the Covered Bazaar where they are sold.

CALLIGRAPHY. There is undoubtedly a grain of truth in the proverb that says 'The Koran came down from Heaven to Mecca and Medina, but it was written in Istanbul.' Throughout the Islamic world, calligraphy—literally 'beautiful writing'—has always been seen as the supreme art, inasmuch as it preserves and

transmits the message of God and the words of the Prophet. It was in Turkey that calligraphy reached its zenith.

Islamic calligraphy has evolved continuously over the centuries in Turkey. Many styles of writing have been developed in the search for greater and greater fluidity. These range from the rectilinear lines of the Kufic style, to a more flowery, intricate Kufic, and then to a cursive style in which letters are intertwined to create the most varied patterns and motifs. Calligraphic styles were also influenced by notable calligraphers such as the poet Yakut, who invented the *tevkii* and *rika* styles, and, in particular, Şeik Hamdullah, who lived in the fifteenth century and is often presented as the father of Ottoman calligraphy. A number of great calligraphers who were responsible for creating one or more of the 54 styles in the repertoire remain, however, unknown to us.

The art of calligraphy, essentially a religious art, is inevitably best represented by the illuminated Korans, but it is also found on the walls of houses and mosques, on precious dishes, and on a wide variety of materials including paper, wood, ceramic and glass. However it is not only a religious art. One of the original features of Ottoman calligraphy was the art of the *tuğra*, the sultan's monogram which all official documents issued by the divan had to bear as a seal guaranteeing their authenticity. Their creators, the *nisancı*, were important figures at court, and sometimes, in addition to being accomplished artists, they were also jurists and theologians. Over the centuries, the composition of the *tuğras* became increasingly sophisticated. Black ink was abandoned in favour of gold, red and blue, and ornamental features

began to appear in the form of branches, clouds, shells and flowers.

There are few interiors in Istanbul where you will not find some calligraphy. Sometimes antique, sometimes contemporary, calligraphic panels are usually hung at eye-level as a sign of respect. This extraordinary art form is still taught. In addition to an extensive knowledge of the many different styles, it also requires a good hand and humility. Major calligraphy artists are now emerging, in response to the demand created by the growing number of public and private collections.

EMBROIDERY. Turkish embroidery is a captivating field, with its innumerable nuances of colour, offset by motifs in gold and silver thread. The finest examples were created to decorate the sultans' palaces, their clothes and those of their retinue, and are now carefully preserved in Istanbul's museums.

From the sixteenth century, freed from geometric designs, Ottoman embroidery burst into flower. The passion for flowers reached its height during the Tulip Period at the start of the eighteenth century. It is true that tulips began to feature in embroidery at this point, but so did violets, hyacinths, dog roses, cherry-blossom and pomegranate flowers. Complete flowers or fragments of flowers were embroidered onto belts, scarves and the edges of towels, while shirts and other items of clothing were decorated with vertical strips of embroidery, and raised patterning in gold. The multi-coloured embroideries used on household linen were generally executed in cross-stitch. Chain-stitch motifs and gold embroideries on cotton, wool and velvet were executed using

hand-drawn patterns. Like miniatures, they feature green trees, luxuriant gardens and lawns dotted with marigolds and narcissi—paradisiacal landscapes capable of melting the hardest of hearts.

In the work that they carried out for the court, the guilds of embroiderers, who practised their trade in the sultans' workshops under the aegis of the seraglio, combined this *point-compté* proliferation of vegetation with openwork, silver droplets and gold purl. They were as likely to embroider tents as kaftans, garden canopies, uniforms and banners. The thread used often came from the harems, where silkworms were lovingly bred to provide the silk for all this finery. But fine embroidery was not only reserved for the palaces. In

Heat and steam are not the only indispensable elements in a *hamam*. An atmosphere of peace and calm is necessary for complete relaxation. In the Küçük Mustafa Paşa Hamamı, soft light, gentle colours and a laid-back attendant create an oasis of serenity in the heart of the city. In the changing cubicle there is room for two bathers to stretch out, drink a tea or a coffee, and smoke cigarettes or a water pipe, while at the entrance, in front of a pile of large Bursa damask towels, the attendant dozes (above and right).

The entrance hall, where the bathers are handed their towels by the attendant, is the only part of the *hamam* in which men and women are not segregated. The Küçük Mustafa Paşa Hamamı, built in the early sixteenth century by the Grand Vizier of Sultan Beyazıt II, is one of the oldest and grandest baths in Istanbul. But despite its imposing architecture, the decor is simple, and in the slightly run-down entrance hall a small, pretty marble basin provides the only note of refinement (left).

The peeling paintwork by the stairs leading down to the Küçük Mustafa Paşa Hamamı, possibly caused by steam infiltrating the walls, gives the entrance a shabby appearance. No matter, for it is here that one leaves the street and enters the *hamam*, a secret world far from the hurly-burly of the city (above). The architecture and layout of the *hamam* in Ortaköy, a suburb on the European shore of the Bosporus, is different from the other sixteenth-century baths designed by Sinan. Instead of having the customary large, domed, cruciform steam-room, it has four separate but identical sections, each topped by a dome, a layout reminiscent of older and smaller *hamams*. The large chandelier and wooden gallery in the central hall are recent additions (right). In Istanbul few old *hamams* have maintained their original decor.

Shafts of light enter the impressive steam-room of the Küçük Mustafa Paşa Hamamı through small glazed skylights, piercing the darkness to illuminate the marble slabs below. Part of the magic of every *hamam* lies in the subtle interplay of light and shade (above and opposite page).

every family women embroidered silk and girls would start preparing their trousseaus at a very early age. Veils, dresses, blouses, bedspreads and mirror-drapes—all of these were embroidered with floral motifs.

Towards the end of the nineteenth century, this proliferation of flowers was complicated by baroque and rococo influences that bordered on mannerism. Nowadays the classic designs have come back into fashion and it is these that provide the inspiration for today's embroiderers. The embroidery school at the Olgunlasma Institute near Taksim teaches the classic tradition, but in a modernized, more stylized version. Evening dresses, table cloths, bags and hand-

kerchiefs are still lavishly embroidered with gold and silver thread and bear witness to the talent of this latest generation of embroiderers.

THE HAMAM. In the subdued light that filters through the skylights, glistening on the marble and hanging in the steam-laden air, you surrender your naked body first to the heat, then to the hands of a masseur and finally to the beneficial effects of water. To purify yourself and to relax: these are the sensual pleasures provided, since antiquity, by Istanbul's *hamams*.

The *hamams* are descendants of the Roman baths, with which they have obvious architectural affinities. Nothing remains, unfortunately,

In the Küçük Mustafa Paşa
Hamamı, a *hamam* which is
simultaneously monumental and
charming, the delicate beauty of
the decorative elements is
heightened by the fact that they
are half-hidden. This superb
floor is made of polychrome
marble (left), while this graceful
fountain is topped by a cupola in
the shape of a seashell (above).

of the city's Byzantine baths, but the Ottoman tradition of baths is very much alive today. In the eighteenth century, Istanbul boasted 150 public *hamams*, not counting those of the various palaces and numerous private baths. This proliferation was due in part to the piety of Istanbulites: for a believer it was as praiseworthy to make a gift of a *hamam* as it was to build a mosque. The *hamam* was a traditional fea-

ture among the outbuildings of the mosque, as in the case of the Süleymaniye.

More than a hundred Ottoman *hamams* are still in use today, often by Istanbulites who have no bathrooms and are expected to present themselves for Friday prayers washed from head to toe. Formerly a social place of leisure in an otherwise secluded life, the baths are still frequented by women who are practising Muslims and who want to purify themselves or by women seeking a cure (the *hamam* is sometimes known as the 'dumb doctor' in recognition of its reputed healing properties).

However, for many devotees the *hamam* remains above all one of life's pleasures, a place where one's body undergoes an initial assault then is gradually brought into a state of pleasurable well-being. The bathers first undress in the *camekân*, or changing room, where they are wrapped in a large towel. From here they enter the *hararet*, or steam-room, where their bodies are subjected to the intense heat of the steam. Then one of the bath attendants takes hold of them, soaps them, scrubs them with a horsehair glove, then massages, stretches them and generally pulls them about. After this thorough massage, the bathers then wash themselves at a cold water fountain, before rinsing and going to stretch out in the *soğukluk*, a room with a more moderate temperature where they can relax and enjoy some delicious sweet or savoury dish, order a coffee or cold drink, and smoke a hookah. By now, totally relaxed and filled with a feeling of well-being, bathers feel almost reborn.

There are too many ambiguities in this whole process—the shared nudity, the contact of bodies, the pleasure of anticipation—for one not to consider a session at a *hamam* as a sensual, if not carnal pleasure. The truth is that, in Istanbul as elsewhere, a *hamam* is what the bather makes of it: religious purification, bodily care, complete physical and mental relaxation, or a more ambiguous pleasure. But whatever the motive, when they finally emerge from a *hamam* the bathers feel happy and clean for all eternity.

Since earliest times, the Ottoman tradition of steam baths has developed hand in hand with the various associated crafts. A standard layout emerged, usually cruciform, and a specific architecture, with arches and cupolas pierced by narrow skylights. The heating sys-

At the Kılıç Ali Paşa Hamamı
in the Tophane neighbourhood,
the copper dishes have been replaced
by plastic ones, but their shape and
function have not changed. The
wearing of a towel is obligatory. They
are generally changed six times

in the course of a bath, which lasts,
on average, for about an hour (above).
How many towels, bars of soap,
dishes and stools have come into
contact with this marble basin (right)?
Over the centuries, even the
stonework in the city's *hamams* has
become worn with age.
Only the water seems eternal.

tem was gradually perfected, involving, as in Roman baths, the circulation of hot air under the floor. There was also the development of particular styles of embroidery used for bath towels. The sophisticated and skilful handiwork reflects the importance of the towel's functions: the custom of displaying the bride's trousseau, the laying out of the towels before the bridal bath, and religious requirements governing ablutions. The towels were often embroidered with rose designs, symbolizing the family, and with propitiatory motifs designed to protect one from the jinn that were thought to lurk in dark corners of the *hamam*. The towels used by men were also often embroidered, but here the motifs tended to be more masculine: agricultural tools set against the background of a field; steamships on wavy seas, depicted Chinese-style; firearms interwoven with country scenes.

Of the remaining beautiful *hamams*, many have been restored to their former glory. One of the eight baths in Istanbul which can be attributed with certainty to the architect Sinan is the *hamam* which Süleyman the Magnificent commissioned from him in 1556 for his wife Haseki Hürrem, also known as Roxelana. Located between Haghia Sofia and the Blue Mosque, on the spot where the best-known of the Byzantine baths used to stand, this splendid *hamam* today houses a salesroom for kilims and carpets. Near the Egyptian Market is the enormous Tahtakale Hamamı, which dates from 1541 and is one of the earliest Ottoman baths in Istanbul. It was disused for a long time, before becoming a tobacco warehouse and later a sausage factory. After restoration, which took five years, it was converted into a

fine covered bazaar. Other old *hamams* have been restored to their original function, such as the very old Küçük Mustafa Paşa Hamamı located close to Aya Kapi, the Holy Gate, one of two gates still visible in the walls along the Golden Horn. The ingenious overlapping of its domes indicates that it dates from the beginning of the sixteenth century. Rarely has a *hamam* been conceived on such a grand scale,

and it is one of the most popular baths, with its spacious changing cubicles and rest rooms, and its *halvets*, cubicles arranged along beautiful wooden galleries where bathers drape themselves in large coloured towels. In Eminönü stands one of Istanbul's most famous *hamams*, the Cağaloğlu, a double bath with one part reserved for men, and the other for women. These baths were a gift to the city in 1741 from Sultan Mehmet I and up until the end of the Ottoman Empire the income from the Cağaloğlu baths was allocated to the library founded by Mehmet and housed in the Haghia Sophia. The crowning glory of this *hamam* is its magnificent steam-room. Its cruciform layout is

The beauty of the Kılıç Ali Paşa Hamamı, built in 1580 and designed by Sinan (opposite page and below), resides in its simple, functional architecture. The central platform, like the steam-room itself, is hexagonal and is surrounded by six arches.

This layout is similar to that of the two *hamams* in Bursa, which date from the thirteenth century. Stretched out on heated marble floor, one can enjoy the three basic elements of a bath—sweating, relaxation and massage by one of the *tellâks*, or bath attendants.

crowned by a dome supported on columns, beneath which lies a splendid marble slab where Franz Liszt and the Emperor Wilhelm have once stretched out for a massage. Of the old *hamams* that are still in use, one should also mention the Kiliç Ali Paşa Hamamı, built by Sinan in 1580, directly opposite the Tophane fountain. It was built to an unusual layout for a Calabrian who had converted to Islam and had then become admiral of Selim II's fleet. Also of note is one of the finest examples from the classical era, the Çemberlitaş Hamamı, located in the neighbourhood of the same name near the Covered Bazaar, and designed in 1583 by the wife of Selim II, Nur Banu. Its main feature is its square steam-room, with a dome supported by columns. Each of the small fountain rooms where one goes to wash is topped with a cupola. Most of its doors are carved in the form of a *mihrab*—a reminder of the religious function of the *hamam*, that of purifying the body before prayer. The Çemberlitaş Hamamı was originally a double bath, but the women's section had to be demolished when an adjacent road was widened. Consequently men and women now have to attend on alternate days (in *hamams* where there is insufficient space for separate sections for men and women, a piece of cloth is hung at the entrance to indicate whose day it is). Many of the other old *hamams* do not have the architectural refinement and splendour of these two, but they are nevertheless very popular: for example the *hamam* at Galatasaray, close to the *lycée* which for many years educated Turkey's French-speaking elite.

Places of purification they may have been, but they were also places of sensual pleasure, and in the royal palaces there was no reason

for the *hamams* not to be as richly appointed as the harems. Embroidered silks, colourful ceramics and gold shone and glistened in the steamy vapours, as the sultan and his dignitaries on one side and their wives and children on the other, lounged naked on the marble slabs. Splendour and nakedness went hand in hand in this dreamy world of the 'Turkish bath', at once luxurious and sensual, exotic and erotic. It was an environment that captured the imagination of many European artists from Ingres onwards.

Topkapı Palace had as many as 30 baths. The double bath designed by Sinan for the sultan and his mother gives us a vivid impression of the luxury of these small palaces of water and marble, palaces in which refinement went

At the *hamam* in Cağaloğlu, the elegance of this delicately sculpted fountain is framed by a marble door with its splendid lintel (right). Some of Istanbul's older *hamams*, and particularly those in the sultans' palaces, are graced by superb metalwork and sculpture. In the double bath built by Sinan at Topkapı, for example, these two baroque taps, made of finely chased *tombak* and cleverly linked by a mixer, provided the sultan with water at just the right temperature (below).

In the double bath at Topkapı a corridor links the men's and women's sections of the bath. The two halves, which are almost identical, were heated from the same heat source. The walls are made of marble and the copper grilles over the windows allowed you a glimpse of the shadow of the most illustrious of bathers washing at the most beautiful of fountains. In the early eighteenth century, Lady Montagu, wife of the English ambassador, was much taken with one of these palace *hamams*, that of the Grand Vizier. In a letter to the Abbé Conti in May 1718, she wrote: 'But no part of it pleased me better than the apartments destined for the *bagnios*. There are two built in exactly the same manner, one answering the other; the baths, fountains and pavements are all of white marble, the roofs gilt, and the walls covered with ceramics; adjoining there are two rooms, and an upper section divided into a *sofa*; in the four corners water falls from shell to shell of white marble from the ceiling to the lower end of the room, where it is collected into a large basin surrounded with pipes that throw up great jets of water as high as the room. The walls are in the form of lattices and on the outside of them planted vines and woodbines form a sort of green tapestry which lends an agreeable obscurity to these delightful chambers.'

All that is left of the interior of the Çirağan Palace, built in 1874 by the Bosporus, is the 'neo-Ottoman' *hamam*, which has now become a major feature of the Çirağan Palace Hotel (below and opposite page).

hand in hand with simplicity. The marble walls of the room where they undressed were hung with richly embroidered fabrics set with pearls. The benches and sofas were covered with embroidered cushions and the sultan would have been served coffee in a silver-gilt coffee-set inlaid with precious stones. In the steam-room, the most beautiful part of the *hamam*, the brilliant white walls and the copper taps with their golden reflections were enveloped in steam, while from a fountain behind a *tombak* grill, boiling water cascaded into a marble bathtub.

During the nineteenth century, sumptuous *hamams* were built in all the new royal palaces along the Bosporus. The sultans' taste for European luxury expressed itself in a frenzy of baroque and rococo decors and this new passion inevitably influenced the design of baths. Mirrors, walls of veined alabaster, plasterwork columns and corniches, domes of coloured glass giving a slightly unreal light—all these elements give the bath built for Abdül Mecit in the Dolmabahçe Palace something of a resemblance to a comic opera stage set. In this cluttered decor, bathers did not need the steam to hide their naked bodies. Similar baths were built in the palaces of Beylerbeyi, Yıldız and Çirağan. All that remains of the latter, built in 1874 for Abdül Aziz and subsequently gutted by fire, is the original shell, which has been incorporated into Istanbul's most luxurious hotel, the Çirağan Palace Hotel. The Çirağan *hamam* is the only one in the city which gives visitors an accurate impression of the legendary delights which the sultans enjoyed in their baths. Presidents Mitterrand and Bush have both stayed in this hotel but we do not know whether they experienced the luxurious and infinite sense of well-being offered by the *hamam*, soothing body and mind alike, and without which no trip to Istanbul is complete.

Ottoman baroque reached new heights of sophistication in the nineteenth-century Dolmabahçe Palace, designed by the Armenian architects Karabet and Nikoğos Balyan. Its *hamam* is built of Egyptian onyx, every inch of which is carved with intricate ornamentation. Daylight floods in through a glazed ceiling protected by a heavy grille. Its basins are decorated with a mass of carved flowers and foliage (left and above), but none of this prevented Sultan Abdül Mecit from enjoying the simple and refined pleasures of the traditional *hamams*: 'What a voluptuous feeling it must be,' wrote Théophile Gautier, after visiting the bath, 'to lie on these slabs, that are as translucent as agate, and to abandon one's relaxed limbs to the expert ministrations of the *tellâks*, in the midst of a cloud of perfumed steam, under a rain of water, rose water and balsam!'

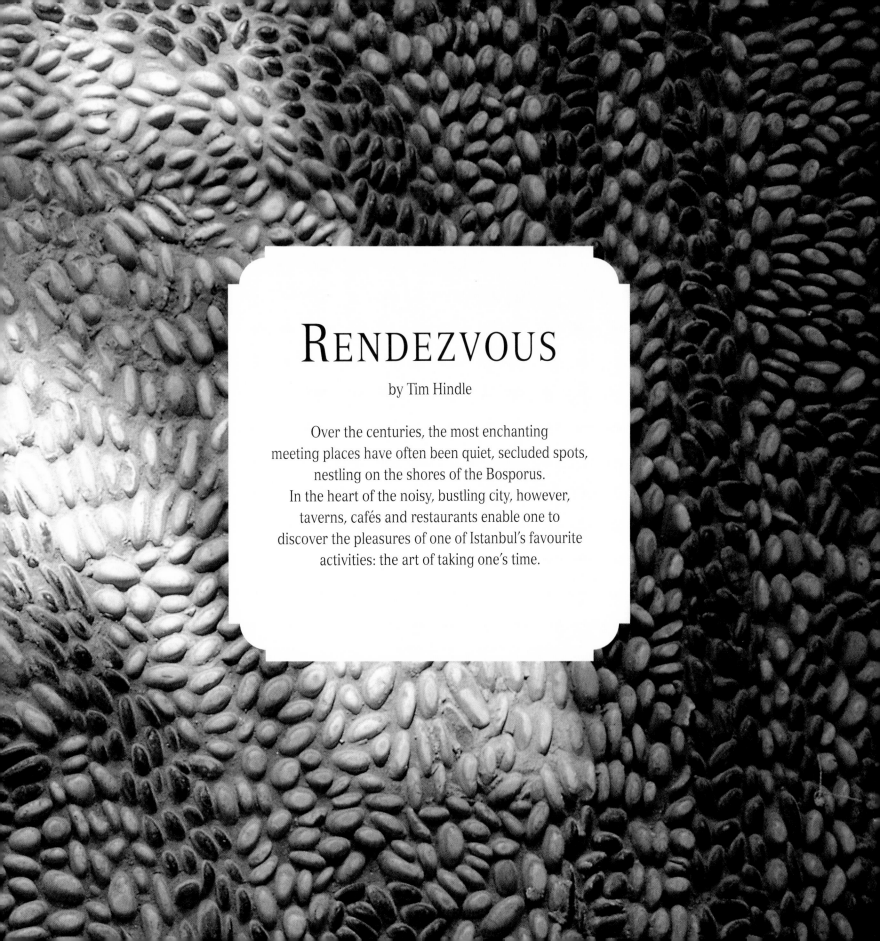

RENDEZVOUS

by Tim Hindle

Over the centuries, the most enchanting
meeting places have often been quiet, secluded spots,
nestling on the shores of the Bosporus.
In the heart of the noisy, bustling city, however,
taverns, cafés and restaurants enable one to
discover the pleasures of one of Istanbul's favourite
activities: the art of taking one's time.

Istanbul sits on one of the most extraordinary geographical locations on earth. It is a cliché to call it the bridge between Europe and Asia, but the cliché is so apt that it is unavoidable. Look at it on a map and see how it lies at the very spot where Europe gently bumps against Asia. Fly out of the city on a clear day and you can see the Bosporus spread out below. Yet, seen from the air, how small this famous waterway seems.

For most of recorded time, this 'bridge' has been man's arterial highway between Europe and Asia. Travellers from one to the other have been funnelled into this small space like the migrating storks that darken the skies over Istanbul on their passage to and from Europe and Africa or the Middle East.

The constant comings and goings of people have, over the centuries, shaped Istanbul's social structure and its meeting places. Indeed, crowds have played a key role in shaping the city's topography almost since the day in AD 326 when Constantine I first traced out the limits of the new capital. The hippodrome, a vast amphitheatre that hosted chariot races and other popular events of the time, could seat 100,000 people. There are few stadia of that size anywhere in the world today.

The residents of Istanbul, who spend their lives in the midst of this constant bustle, naturally devote a lot of time and energy to creating havens of peace. These places are designed to shut out the travellers and help to bind the city's hard core of permanence together.

For this reason, Istanbul is not an easy city to discover. Unlike many other cities, it does not have a broad boulevard where the locals strut and promenade and where the traveller can sit and soak up the atmosphere before setting off to explore. There is no obvious place for the traveller to visit first, no landmark to which all other places relate, such as the Via Veneto, the Champs-Élysées or Piccadilly Circus. Istanbulites like to meet in places which are half-hidden from the public eye, tucked away down narrow alleys or in courtyards: enclosed spaces where the emphasis is on internal reflection rather than external display.

On reflection, it is not quite true to say that Istanbul has no central landmark to which all other places relate. It has, but it is not a man-made landmark. Rather it is the Bosporus, the natural channel that brings the waters of the tempestuous Black Sea down to the Sea of Marmara, through the Dardanelles and into the calm waters of the Aegean Sea beyond.

Running roughly in a north-south direction, the Bosporus occupies a special place in the hearts of all Istanbulites. For me, it acts like a compass whenever I drive up and down the city's multitude of steep, narrow, cobbled streets. Irregular glimpses of the Bosporus and the towers of the two giant suspension bridges

The footpaths in the gardens and courtyards of mansions and palaces are often decorated with mosaics of small stones (preceding double page). The elegance of breakfast on the balcony at the Çiragan Hotel, overlooking the Bosporus and the marble Çiragan Palace (below). The nineteenth-century rococo building lay in ruins for years until it was lovingly restored as part of the hotel complex. Masons with the necessary skills were hard to find. Under the smooth surface of every great hotel lie hours and hours of skilled but unseen labour. At the Çiragan, the tables in the hotel's different restaurants are laid with the greatest of care (right).

After three days travelling by train, the passengers on the Orient Express would be taken to the Pera Palas hotel, which was built by the Compagnie des wagons-lits in 1892 for their benefit. The hotel, with its impressive lounges, marble decor, dark woodwork, and its monumental lift, is like a museum, and staying there is always a fascinating experience (left). The doorman has seen people from all over the world pass through the doors of the hotel. The names of some of the best-known guests are inscribed in brass plaques above the doors of the rooms: Ernest Hemingway, Trotsky, Sarah Bernhardt, Greta Garbo (above).

Çelik Gülersoy, head of the Turkish
Touring and Automobile Club (below).
Nobody has done more to restore
Istanbul's architectural heritage. One
of his greatest successes is the restored

Khedive's summer palace (Hidiv Kasri)
on the Asian shore of the Bosporus. It
is largely thanks to Mr Gülersoy that
this building, covered in wisteria
(below right), is a popular place
among Istanbulites for tea (above
right) or receptions.

that cross it guide me when I lose my bearings.

For centuries, some of the city's most enchanting meeting places have been located beside this great waterway or on some hillside with a panoramic view of it. At Küçüksu, on the Asian side, there used to be a famous picnic spot near two small rivers known as the Sweet Waters of Asia. Eighteenth- and nineteenth-century European artists liked to depict these picnics as the epitome of Ottoman sensuality, with picnickers lounging around tasting delicacies and listening to music in elegant rural bliss. An Ottoman princess left a description of this type of party:

'In summer there were moonlight parties by the Bosporus. Veiled in white yashmaks and wrapped in silk cloaks, the ladies would be rowed in long *kayiks* manned by several pairs of oarsmen. Attached to the stern of the *kayik*,

squares of cloth or satin, embroidered in gold or silver and edged with little silver fishes, floated on the waves. Musicians, both players and singers, preceded them in a separate boat, and as the oars dipped rhythmically into the moonlit waters, strains of music were wafted towards the following *kayiks*. It was an accepted custom for many other boats and *kayiks* to accompany the party on the sea, forming a long procession,

The delightfully different bedrooms and bathrooms at the Khedive's summer palace. The bedroom which belonged to the viceroy is decorated with a fabric specially woven in Bursa, the design of which is a copy of the original wall covering. The bed is in the same style as the wardrobes which were found there before restoration. The old bathroom taps are of English origin.

Entellektüel Cavit (below) sitting proudly on the terrace of his tavern in the Çiçek Pasajı, the former flower market which has become a meeting place for thirsty strollers wishing to escape from the bustle of Beyoğlu (right). These delicious *kurabiye* (above), a kind of sweet biscuit covered in powdered sugar, taste best dunked in tea.

the bobbing lanterns attached to the craft shining soft and yellow under the night's brilliant moonlight.'

Today we can get a glimpse of the past at the magnificent Çirağan Palace, which was completed in 1874. The building, which stands on the European shore, was gutted by fire in January 1910. It has recently been restored as part of a luxurious hotel complex, with a swimming pool that seems to merge into the waters of the Bosporus behind. President Bush, the first American president to visit the city for over 30 years, stayed here in 1991, and he can have had few more delightful experiences than taking tea on the hotel's waterfront verandah.

The Çirağan is one of a number of modern hotels in the city—others include the Sheraton, the Divan and the Conrad—involved in a concerted revival of traditional Ottoman cuisine. Many superb dishes were invented in the sybaritic Ottoman court, where several hundred chefs slaved away with no purpose other than to provide excitement for a sultan's jaded palate. For them, time was no object: a single starter, like *çerkez tavuk* (Circassian chicken with ground walnuts and a paprika sauce), could take several hours to prepare.

As well as being tasty, Ottoman dishes tend to be high in protein. Vegetables are usually cooked with a little meat and a soupçon of sugar. Desserts are rich in yoghurts, milk and honey, and may even include finely minced chicken, as in the sweet milk pudding called *tavuk göğsü*.

Yoghurt, made by nomads in the region since long before Christ, is a star ingredient. Manufacturers zealously nurture their cultures as if they were live animals (which in a sense they are), and yoghurt can be used in every course of an Ottoman meal—in soups, *mezes*, salad dressings, on meat and in desserts, as well as in the national drink *ayran* (a mixture of yoghurt, water and salt). But Ottoman cuisine also relies on some more unusual raw materials, like orchid root (taken in a hot drink called *salep*), and rose water (*gül suyu*), which is used to flavour dozens of dishes.

After the fall of the Ottoman empire, these dishes retreated into the home. The visitor to Istanbul who missed an invitation was unlikely to taste the real quality of good Ottoman cuisine. But all that changed in the 1980s, with the growth of a wealthy professional and commercial class demanding higher standards of cuisine. A number of restaurants now serve classic

Drinking tea and smoking hookahs are old social customs in Istanbul. Today they may not occupy as important a place in the lives of Istanbulites as they used to, but each has its own distinctive paraphernalia that has remained more or less unchanged for centuries (right, opposite page, below). 'Nothing is more propitious to poetic reverie than inhaling small mouthfuls of this odorous smoke, which is refreshed by the water it is drawn through and reaches you after having circulated through the morocco pipe, whilst seated on the cushions of a divan . . .' wrote Théophile Gautier in 1852.

aubergine, fish and chicken dishes which surpass the best home cooking.

Some Turkish delicacies, however, can still only be found in private houses or in certain shops. This applies to rose jam, for example, which has the same consistency as the honeys for which Turkey is also rightly famous. You also have to go to the right place if you want to drink a cooling lemonade, which should be made to a recipe which has been handed down through four or five generations. Carefully prepared Turkish coffee—more like a complete course than a drink—can also be hard to find, as can Turkish tea. Personally I find the tea too bitter, but it is always elegantly served, even on a ferry boat rolling up the Bosporus.

As for Turkish delight, the kind found in Istanbul is different from anything passing for Turkish delight outside Turkey. Lightly pow-

dered, its gooey consistency is counterbalanced by the hard pistachio nuts inside. Also worth seeking out is the tasty salted fish known as *lakerda*. Another delicacy is white cheese, which

should spread like margarine and is delicious on bread with a slice of tomato, basil, a pinch of salt and a few drops of the best Turkish olive oil (which comes from around the town of Ayva-

lik). There are few finer breakfasts to be found anywhere.

On the opposite bank of the Bosporus to the Çirağan Palace, further north, are a couple of superb restaurants which take the visitor a step closer to the tradition described by the Ottoman princess, as they have their own private boats to ferry customers across from the European side. Customers for the fashionable Körfez restaurant embark at Rumeli Hisar, the fortress built by the Ottomans during their famous siege of the city in 1452. The waterside terrace at Körfez provides a delightful setting in which to taste one of the restaurant's most unusual specialities: highly prized (and highly priced) sea-bass cooked in a cake of salt.

Good fish can also be enjoyed in many less expensive establishments. The charming Kumpaki area, an old fisherman's quarter

Istanbul can be very hot so much ingenuity has gone into creating cool resting places, such as this shady terrace jutting out into the water at Yıldız Park (opposite page), or this marble kiosk on Çamlıca hill (below left). Even the drinking fountains spouting *ayran*, a refreshing yoghurt drink, like this one at the Yeşil Ev hotel (below), are made of marble.
The heat, however, does not deter Istanbulites from eating spicy foods, such as this *lâhmacun*. Made with hot peppers, onions and mincemeat on a base of unleavened bread, it is the local version of the Italian pizza and tastes best eaten on the street (above).

Restful courtyards abound in this city that itself never seems to be at rest. Here are two of the most delightful: the café located in the gardens of the Archaeological Museum (right), one of the sights that must not be missed; and the courtyard of the Yeşil Ev hotel (below). As elsewhere in the city, the attention to detail is extraordinary. Look, for example, at the magnificent lamp-posts at the Yeşil Ev hotel, where the immaculately decorated rooms look out onto the dome and minarets of the Blue Mosque.

behind the mosque of Sultan Ahmet I, contains some 50 fish restaurants huddled together in lively, narrow streets. There are also a number of popular fish restaurants around the pretty bay at Tarabya, an old village on the European side. This once elegant area has now become rather seedy and a number of its restaurants are not recommended. Of those, however, that can be, Facyo's is, in my view, consistently the best.

Further up the Bosporus, beyond the Sweet Waters of Asia, is Club 29, the creation of one of the city's foremost restaurateurs, Metin Fadíllíoğlu. Like many of Istanbul's most fashionable meeting places, it has different summer and winter locations and combines club, bar, restaurant, café and disco. You can spend the day reclining by the pool, enjoying what must be one of the most beautiful views in the West, you can simply come for dinner, or you can join the lively crowd of local young people, who gather at midnight for the disco.

Metin's wife Zeynep is a first cousin of Rífat Özbek, the internationally acclaimed fashion designer who was born in Istanbul. Clearly a sense of style runs in the family, for Zeynep has created a place that changes its mood to suit its purpose—chic restaurant, noisy disco, or exclusive club. The club's only aspect looks out onto the Bosporus, with its infinite variations in mood, and the pervading atmosphere, once again, is peaceful and inward-looking.

In winter, Metin and Zeynep move into the heart of the city where they run the disco and restaurant Taxim, a magnet for the owners of fast cars and Özbek dresses. Taxim, designed by Nigel Coates, one of Britain's leading interior designers, has been honed around the concrete pillars of an old factory.

Istanbulites love flowers. Here roses have been decoratively arranged in a marble basin (below). Traditional *objets d'art*, such as the Beykoz decanter and glasses, which here contain refreshing lemonade, as well as simple, everyday objects such as the *cezve* used to prepare coffee, are decorated with floral motifs. But flowers are not merely decorative. Rose water is added to many different kinds of food, such as sorbets and puddings, and old, heavily scented roses, notably *Rosa centifolia*, are used to make delicious rose jam (opposite page).

There are a number of charming places located well back from the Bosporus, high up on the hills that embrace it on its journey from the Black Sea to the Sea of Marmara. I have a special affection for Abdullah's, a traditional Turkish restaurant where my wedding reception was held. It is located in the hills above Emirgan on the European side. It is not an easy place to find, but it has beautiful gardens, a menu of classic Turkish dishes and a view to sigh over.

The highest hill is called Çamlıca. On its summit used to sit a pretty village of wooden houses, which was burnt to the ground early this century, as was so much of Istanbul when gas and electric lighting first came into contact with the city's handsome wooden buildings. Nowadays, Çamlıca is topped by an Ottoman-style pavilion serving classical Turkish dishes. If these sometimes have a failing, it stems from the tendency to add too much oil. The view, however, is breathtaking and the air is cool and fresh.

A more recent building of interest is Hıdıv Kasrı, the Khedive's summer palace. A restored,

Visitors with a sweet tooth will particularly enjoy Istanbul. The *lokum*, or Turkish delight, being prepared in this old shop in the Galatasaray district of the city is unlike any found outside Turkey. The gelatinous cubes coated with powdered sugar are flavoured with rose water. And what do they contain, these four pots that seem to be chatting to each other on the shelves of the same shop? Hidden modestly under their cloth covers are delicious home-made jams, at least one of which is certain to contain . . . rose water.

Pandeli's restaurant is an old favourite of discerning locals, and lunch is the best time to catch up on local gossip. The blue tiles (above) add to the coolness of the little rooms, which are reached by a steep, narrow, stone staircase. The *börek* at Pandeli's are renowned. Here, the light pastry triangles are being prepared with a typical cheese and herb filling. When lightly fried, they swell up and turn temptingly brown.

turn-of-the-century art nouveau palace, it originally belonged to the Turkish viceroy of Egypt when the Ottomans ruled Egypt in the nineteenth century. Draped in a magnificent wisteria, the palace has been converted into a small hotel of great character. Its restaurant, which provides live Turkish music for its guests, draws many Istanbulites to this out-of-the-way location.

The Khedive's summer palace is one of a number of old buildings in Istanbul which have been lovingly restored in recent years, most of them by an organization called the Turkish Touring and Automobile Club, to which the city owes a great debt of gratitude. The club's best-known restoration is the Yeşil Ev, or the Green House, a charming oasis of peace not far from the Blue Mosque and Haghia Sophia.

The Yeşil Ev is a small establishment, closer in style to an English country house than a city centre hotel. Behind the hotel is a cool courtyard café where a fountain plays and the sunlight is dappled by the shade of linden trees, creating an atmosphere far removed from the frenetic tourism going on just beyond the front door.

Around Yeşil Ev, in the heart of the Ottoman city, the Turkish art of creating peace amid swirling activity finds its highest expression. The impact of the Archaeological Museum is made

all the more powerful by the stillness and cool shade of the café there, with its chairs and tables scattered casually among the ancient sculptures. (Incidentally, the Lycian sarcophagi, with their reliefs of horses' heads, are for me one of the greatest works of art in the world.)

Whenever I am in this part of Istanbul around lunchtime I invariably head for Pandeli's. Its cool, blue-tiled atmosphere has long provided welcome respite from the noise and crowds of the surrounding markets and ferry terminals. Finding it is not easy and many first time visitors have had cause to wonder what lies at the top of the steep stone stairs leading to its first-floor premises. The climb is worth it, however. The menu is wide-ranging, and features many excellent Turkish dishes. I would particularly recommend, as a starter, some cold aubergine salad and warm *börek* (delicious local cheeses and herbs in wafer-thin pastry). Do not, however, become so absorbed in the food that you forget to look around you: the clientele at Pandeli's is often local and always interesting, reflecting the extraordinary mix of cultures and religions to which this city has, at one time or another, been home.

Yeşil Ev and Pandeli's are pleasant places to stop off at when visiting the magnificent Topkapi Palace and the surrounding sights. Two other

Today there is a new side to life in Istanbul. Papillon (left and opposite page) and Taxim (below) have bold, extrovert interiors and are typical of a new type of restaurant and bar frequented by affluent young Turks. Taxim's use of the letter 'x' instead of Turkish letters to represent the sound 'ks' is indicative of the Western influence behind such places.

interesting areas with a wealth of excellent bars and restaurants are Beyoğlu and Nişantaşı, both of which are situated on the other side of the Golden Horn. Beyoğlu is synonymous with nineteenth- and early twentieth-century Istanbul. It has been carefully restored in recent years and the old, red and white trams have returned to the main thoroughfare, which is now closed to traffic. For me, Beyoğlu will always be linked to three places in particular: the Pera Palas hotel, the Galatasaray Turkish bath (or *hamam*) and the Çiçek Pasajı (the Flower Arcade).

The Pera Palas hotel evokes the ghosts of exotic espionage. Mata Hari, Agatha Christie and Kemal Atatürk are among its famous guests, and it is easy to imagine spies with romantic Balkan names skulking behind the marble columns. Today the hotel lacks a bit of polish, but it is worth seeing for its *fin de siècle* architecture

and for the cakes in its coffee shop next door.

Turkish baths are an ancient social ritual, the purpose of which is to relax and tone up the body. They are discreet places where the sexes are segregated. Many Turks still remember being taken by their grandmothers to the local

In summer, what could be more pleasant than to watch the day drawing to a close, whilst reclining comfortably on the cushions at Club 29 on the Asian shore of the Bosporus (right). Gentle light from the flickering flames of the club's candles (below) gradually replaces the fierce brightness of the sun. These candelabra greet the guests who arrive by sea and line the steps which lead up from the Bosporus.

hamam, where they spent the morning washing, chatting and drinking tea. No self-respecting new hotel in Istanbul is now complete without its own *hamam*, but, in my experience, modern baths are too bright and antiseptic, lacking the hazy atmosphere essential to this traditional meeting place. Istanbul's most famous *hamam* is at Cağaloğlu, but the Galatasaray *hamam* in the backstreets of Beyoğlu is a livelier place, and its massage is less vigorous.

The Çiçek Pasajı is a curious arcade full of *meyhane* (taverns) whose tables spill out onto the passageway. The taverns all offer similar fare, but Entellektüel Cavit's place is popular with the locals. If you are lucky, you will see Madame Anahit, an elderly Armenian lady, playing a few golden oldies on her accordion, and you are bound to stumble across somebody you have already met in Beyoğlu.

Nişantaşı is a largely residential area where a number of modern cafés and bars have sprung up, and where, at a price, you can buy European *haute couture*. The best restaurant in

the area is the Park Samdan, the flagship of the Samdan group which was created by Ahmet Çapa, the former partner of Metin Fadíllíoğlu but now his big rival. As is the way, a number of good restaurants have been started by former employees of Ahmet and Metin. Such is the case with the fashionable Sans, a restaurant that has recently become almost more 'in' than the Park Samdan.

A number of coffee shops and bars have opened to serve the chic shoppers of Nişantaşı. My favourite is Zihni's, which is usually extremely noisy but vibrantly alive. An area which rivals Nişantaşı for modern restaurants and bars is the district of Etiler, where the main

street is lined with good places to go. This is where Club 29 moves to in the winter and it is also home to Papillon, a restaurant that started out as a pizzeria, but which has recently grown into one of the city's most popular bars.

Most of these modern establishments are the antithesis of a typical traditional Istanbul rendezvous. Peace and tranquility are not the object, and the uniformity of their fashion-conscious clientele is in stark contrast to the rich ethnic mix which for centuries formed the core of old Istanbul. For myself, I prefer places like Pandeli's and the Pera Palas, places which give the visitor the feeling of penetrating right into the heart of the city.

The architecture of Club 29 is inspired by the Villa Hadriana in Rome.
The statues by the swimming pool (above) are copies of statues in the Archaeological Museum.
The finely embroidered curtains of this window, with the light of the Bosporus breaking through the shutters behind, bear witness to the richness of Istanbul's past, a past of which Istanbulites are increasingly proud.

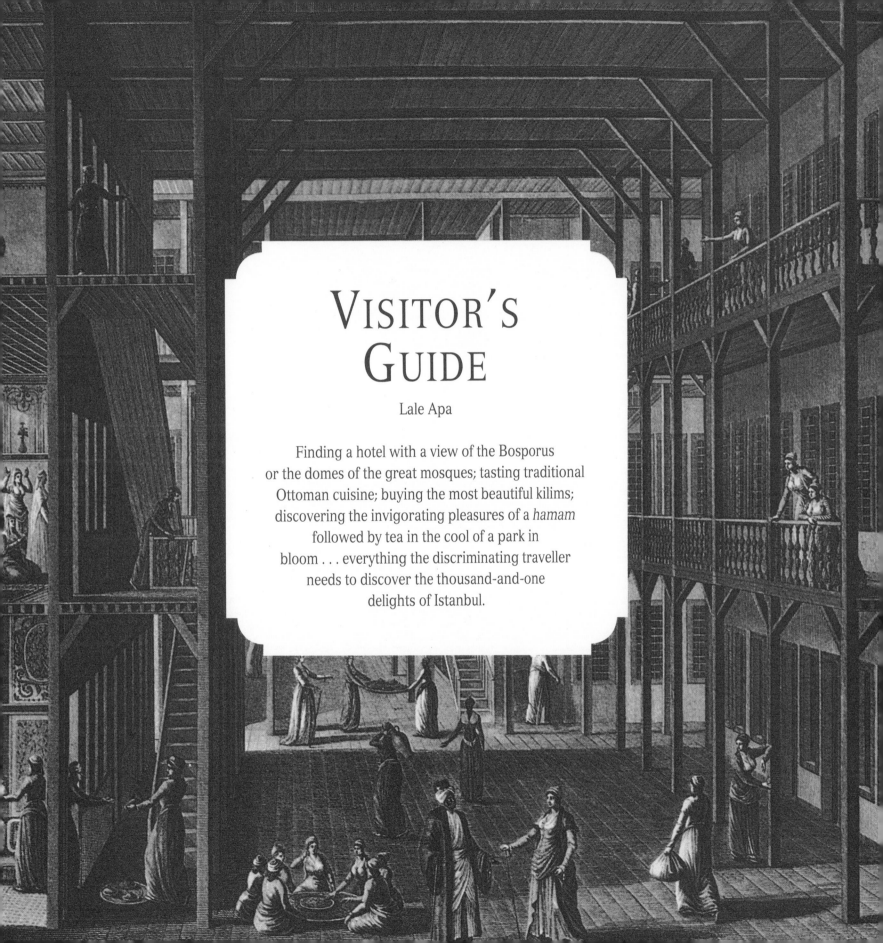

VISITOR'S GUIDE

Lale Apa

Finding a hotel with a view of the Bosporus
or the domes of the great mosques; tasting traditional
Ottoman cuisine; buying the most beautiful kilims;
discovering the invigorating pleasures of a *hamam*
followed by tea in the cool of a park in
bloom . . . everything the discriminating traveller
needs to discover the thousand-and-one
delights of Istanbul.

The addresses in this visitor's guide have been researched by Krysia Bereday Burnham in Istanbul, under the supervision of Lale Apa. In addition to the hotels, restaurants, cafés and shops mentioned or photographed in the book, we have included a number of other places recommended to us by those Istanbulites who have kindly opened their doors to the authors. The addresses of places mentioned in the book are cross-referenced to the relevant pages.

The entries are classified under headings and each address includes, in capital letters, the relevant district or village on the Bosporus, in order to help readers locate them on the map and plan their itineraries.

Inter-city codes throughout Turkey have been changed as of January 1994. Istanbul's code is (212) for the European side of the Bosporus (for numbers beginning with 2, 5, or 6), and (216) for the Asian side (for numbers beginning with 3 or 4). You must also use these codes when calling one side from the other, but no code is necessary within the same side of the city. When calling from abroad, dial 90 (the country code for Turkey) followed by the number.

The guide is illustrated with engravings by A. I. Melling, Sultan Selim III's architect and his sister Sultana Hadidge's draughtsman. They were published in Paris in 1819 in a book entitled Voyage Pittoresque de Constantinople et des rives du Bosphore (Picturesque travels in Constantinople and on the banks of the Bosporus). For captions to these illustrations see Credits, p. 256.

PALACES

Aynalikavak
Kasimpaşa , HASKÖY
Tel.: (212) 250 40 94
A delightful little pavilion dating from the eighteenth century is set in the midst of a largely industrial district on the northern shore of the Golden Horn. Visitors should check whether the restoration of the building has been completed.

Beylerbeyi
Çayirbasi Duraği, BEYLERBEYI
Tel.: (216) 321 93 20
(see pp. 146, 147, 160-163, 170, 171)
This white marble summer palace, which forms a perfect counterpoint to the elaborate Dolmabahçe, is situated on the Asian bank of the Bosporus. It has a harem, ornamental lakes and windows that might look familiar to some, for the Empress Eugénie of France had them copied for the Tuileries Palace in Paris. Coffee is available in the grounds.

Dolmabahçe
BEŞIKTAŞ
Tel.: (212) 258 55 44
(see pp. 10, 11, 149-155, 212, 213)
Built in 1856, this is the grandest of the sultans' palaces in Istanbul. Dolmabahçe ('the overflowing garden') is flanked by a 600-metre-long marble quay and has hundreds of reception rooms where Bohemian glass chandeliers, huge Hereke carpets and mixture of Ottoman and European furniture never fail to dazzle visitors.

Göksu
KÜÇÜKSU
Tel.: (216) 332 33 03
(see pp. 15, 148)
An elegant sultans' summer residence, built in the nineteenth century. The beautiful baroque fountain is not to be missed.

Ilhamur
Ilhamurdere Caddesi, BEŞIKTAŞ
Tel.: (212) 261 29 91
(see p. 14)
This nineteenth-century folly owes its name, which means 'the river of lime trees', to the trees which used to surround and shade it. The grounds, which include a marvellous ornamental lake, are a delightful haven right in the centre of the city. The perfect place for tea in the late afternoon.

Maslak
Büyükdere Caddesi, MASLAK
Tel.: (212) 276 10 22
A charming imperial Ottoman lodge decorated with elegance in the nineteenth century. The café in the camellia conservatory is particularly pleasant.

Şale Köşkü
Yıldız Park, entrance on the coastal road between BEŞIKTAŞ and ORTAKÖY.
Tel.: (212) 261 20 43
(see pp. 156-160)
This nineteenth-century Swiss chalet in Yıldız Park is surrounded by pavilions of many different styles. The visitor will no doubt be charmed by its mother-of-pearl doors and by Abdül Hamit II's furniture, some of which was carved by the sultan himself. The calm of the gardens is another welcome feature (cf. Cafés, p. 247).

MUSEUMS

Akbank Kültür Sanat Eğitim Merkezi
BEYOĞLU
Tel.: (212) 252 35 03, 252 35 04
This cultural and artistic association is established on the premises of a major bank. It is a meeting place for Istanbul art lovers on the look-out for the latest western trends. The association holds monthly exhibitions of works by Turkish and foreign artists.

Archaeological Museum
SULTANAHMET
Tel.: (212) 520 77 40
In 1993 this museum was named European Museum of the Year by the Council of Europe. It fully deserves this honour, for it contains one of the world's finest collections of Graeco-Roman antiquities, including some remarkable sarcophagi, together with antiquities from the first two millenia of Byzantium and Constantinople.

Feshane
Defterdar Vapur Iskele Caddesi, Haliç Kıyısı, EYÜP
Tel.: (212) 258 32 12
This one-time fez factory on the right bank of the Golden Horn has recently been restored and transformed into an impressive complex by the talented Italian architect, Gae Aulenti. It will be used for exhibitions of modern art, conferences and shows of private collections. The pharmaceutical company Eczacibasi contributed to the project.

Galata Mevlevihane
Galip Dede Sokak 13-15, TÜNEL
Tel.: (212) 245 41 41
This tekke, or dervish monastery, houses a museum of musical instruments, costumes, prayer rugs and other artefacts used by the whirling dervishes. Ceremonies with ritual music and dance are held on the last Sunday of every month.

Military Museum
(Askeri Müze)
HARBIYE
Tel.: (212) 232 16 98
Besides weaponry, this museum contains a wonderful collection of costumes and richly embroidered tents.

Museum of Calligraphy
Beyazıt Meydanı
Tel.: (212) 527 58 51
(see pp. 188, 189)
Housed in the medrese (Muslim school) of the Beyazidiye mosque complex, this museum is the only one of its kind in the world. It has a remarkable collection of rare books, manuscripts and calligraphic inscriptions dating from the second half of the eighteenth century to the present day.

Museum of Carpets and Kilims
Near the Blue Mosque, SULTANAHMET
Tel.: (212) 528 53 32
According to one expert, 'This museum makes one want to go out and buy a carpet', which is not far from the truth. Will you be able to resist the temptation after seeing this magnificent collection from Turkey's various weaving centres?

Museum of Turkish and Islamic Art
At Meydanı 46, SULTANAHMET
Tel.: (212) 528 51 58
This museum, in the palace built for Ibrahim Paşa in the heart of old Stamboul, is one of the hidden treasures of Istanbul. It contains magnificent carpets and ceramics dating from the fifteenth century. Among other things, the museum shop sells reproductions of old engravings at reasonable prices.

Naval Museum
(Deniz Müzesi)
BEŞIKTAŞ
Tel.: (212) 261 00 40
This is the place to see the long, elegant caïques used by the sultans on the waters of the Bosporus.

Pottery Kiosk
(Çinili Kösk)
SULTANAHMET
Tel.: (212) 520 77 40
This charming kiosk in the grounds of the Archaeological Museum is one of the few surviving buildings dating from the Ottoman conquest. It has a handsome collection of pottery, notably Seljuk and Iznik, and a beautiful fountain with peacocks.

Sadberk Hanım Museum
Büyükdere Caddesi 27-29, SARIYER
Tel.: (212) 242 38 13
(see p. 16)
This museum, created by the Koç family, contains an extensive ethnographic collection ranging from prehistoric stone and glass artefacts to textiles and costumes from antiquity. One room is given over to the traditional henna ceremony and another to the circumcision bed. The museum is housed in a superbly restored yalı by the Bosporus.

Topkapı Palace Museum
SULTANAHMET
Tel.: (212) 512 04 80
(see pp. 166-169)
The famous seat of the Ottoman government and principal residence of the sultans, Topkapı Palace is a place of enormous historical significance and the scene of many an intrigue. Its harem was populated with concubines, odalisques and

eunuchs, and Ottoman princes decided the fate of the empire and received ambassadors from all over the world in its courtyards. The 84-carat diamond and fabulous emeralds in the Treasury are not be missed, nor is the Baghdad Kiosk (Bagdat Kösk), or the manuscripts, costumes, textiles, pottery, crystal and porcelain. One of the largest imperial collections in Europe.

Yapi Kredi Kültür Merkezi
Istiklal Caddesi 285, BEYOĞLU
Tel.: (212) 245 20 41
Turkish banks frequently organize exhibitions of surprising quality and the Cultural Association of the Yapi Kredi is no exception. Situated on the elegant Istiklal Caddesi in the heart of Beyoğlu, it possesses collections of craft objects from the seventeenth century, Turkish silverware, shadow-theatre puppets, and the third-largest collection of sixth-century Roman and Byzantine coins in the world.

HOTELS

Avicenna
Mimar Mehmet Ağa Caddesi, Amiral Tafdil Sokak 31/33, SULTANAHMET
Tel.: (212) 517 05 05
You will probably fall in love with this old blue and white, wooden Ottoman house. Its 36 rooms—some with a view over the Sea of Marmara—are furnished with contemporary furniture and there is a pleasant terrace for breakfast.

Ayasofya Pansionlari
Soğukçesme Sokak
SULTANAHMET
Tel.: (212) 513 36 60
This delightful hotel in a pretty paved street just behind the Haghia Sophia is made up of a series of wooden houses in pastel tones. The rooms have been restored in the style of the period.

Çirağan Palace
Çiragan, BEŞIKTAŞ
Tel.: (212) 258 33 77
(see pp. 6, 39, 210, 211, 216, 217)
This magnificent nineteenth-century palace has recently been converted into a luxury hotel. If you want a room with windows opening onto the Bosphorus, gardens which go right up to the water's edge and Ottoman cuisine, which you can sample in the hotel's

traditional restaurant, the Tuğra, then this is the place for you.

Halı
Klodfarer Caddesi 20, ÇEMBERLITAŞ
Tel.: (212) 516 21 70
You might be surprised by the number of carpets scattered about the hall and the 36 rooms of this hotel, but the name provides a clue, for *halı* means 'carpet'. You will undoubtedly be impressed by the beauty of its white, marble façade and the glorious view over the sea from the terrace.

Hidiv Kasrı
ÇUBUKLU
Tel.: (216) 331 26 51
(see pp. 220, 221)
Once the palace of the Viceroy of Egypt, this early twentieth-century residence was converted into a hotel after many years of neglect. It is one of the most pleasant havens of peace in the city, though it is quite far from the city centre. The rooms are furnished in period style. The fountain surrounded by marble columns at the entrance and the series of reception rooms are reminiscent of a film set, and indeed the hotel frequently receives requests to film there.

Hyatt Regency Hotel
Taskisla, TAKSIM
Tel.: (212) 225 70 00
This latest addition to the city's luxury hotels has sumptuous Turkish and Italian restaurants, a Turkish-style decor and an

extensive business centre. It is very central and the rooms are quiet and elegant.

Ibrahim Paşa
Terzihane Sokak 5, SULTANAHMET
Tel.: (212) 518 03 94
This old house nestling in a corner of the hippodrome has been attractively restored and converted into a small hotel with a view over the Blue Mosque and the Sea of Marmara.

Kariye
Kariye Camii Sokaği 18, EDIRNEKAPI
Tel.: (212) 534 84 14
For anyone interested in history, this hotel is ideally placed, albeit a little far from the centre. It is located near the city walls and the church of Saint Saviour-in-Chora, the most important Byzantine church after Haghia Sophia. The rooms are reasonably priced.

Konuk Evi
Soğukçesme Sokaği, SULTANAHMET
Tel.: (212) 513 36 60
This recently opened hotel, whose name means 'the guest house', is near Haghia Sophia. The latest restoration by Çelik Gülerso, it has a garden and a restaurant in a conservatory.

Pera Palas
Meşrutiyet Caddesi, TEPEBAŞI
Tel.: (212) 251 45 60
(see pp. 218, 219)

The historic and luxurious Pera Palas was built for the passengers of the Orient Express. During the war it became the haunt of spies and princes. Its 139 rooms are decorated with elegant simplicity and have period furniture and plumbing. The hotel bar is still a popular meeting place for Istanbulites.

Splendid Palace
23 Nisan Caddesi, 71 Büyükada, PRINCES' ISLES
Tel.: (216) 382 69 50
This Ottoman-style hotel, once the most prestigious hotel on the Princes' Isles, is in urgent need of restoration. It is well worth a visit, however, if only for the historical interest of the building. Built in 1908, the hotel has 70 rooms, some of which have a marvellous view of the sea. While you are there, make sure you take a trip to the beach by calash.

Sumengen
Mimar Mehmet Ağa Caddesi, Amiral Tafdil Sokak 21, SULTANAHMET
Tel.: (212) 517 68 69
This Ottoman house was restored four years ago. It has been painted a pretty green picked out in white and furnished in the style of the period.

Swissôtel
MAÇKA
Tel.: (212) 259 01 01
This Japanese-owned megalith has luxurious rooms. The decor is modern but bland and there is a

terrace restaurant with a striking view over the Bosporus.

Yesil Ev
Kabasakal Caddesi 5, SULTANAHMET
Tel.: (212) 517 67 85
(see pp. 227, 228, 229)
Situated in the heart of the old town by the Blue Mosque, the Yesil Ev Hotel is in a delightful Ottoman home that has recently been restored. There is a charming garden where you will be unable to resist having tea and the rooms are furnished in period style.

Other recommended big hotels are: the **Sheraton** for its restaurant, the Revan; the **Hilton**, which was the first hotel to appear on the Istanbul skyline; the **Ramada**, in the heart of the old town; the **Istanbul Marmara**, in the heart of Taksim, which has an attractive piano bar with a striking view of Istanbul; the **Divan**, with its elegant, immaculate rooms and excellent restaurant; and the **Mövenpick**, which is relatively new, but close to the business district.

RESTAURANTS

Abdullah
Koru Caddesi 11, EMIRGAN
(see pp. 230)
It is well worth making the effort to find this traditional Turkish restaurant in order to enjoy a memorable meal of classic Turkish dishes in the gardens overlooking the Bosporus.

Address Restaurant
Tamburi Ali Efendi Sokak 11, ETILER
Tel.: (212) 263 14 04
This recently opened and luxuriously decorated restaurant and bar is owned by one of the best restaurateur families, the Çapas. It is Istanbul's first members-only eating rendezvous, though distinguished non-members are also welcome on weekdays if they book well in advance. The menu consists of French, Turkish and Chinese dishes.

Les Ambassadeurs
Cevdet Paşa Caddesi 113-115, BEBEK
Tel.: (212) 263 30 02
Situated in the Bebek Hotel by the Bosporus, this restaurant is frequented by an elegant clientele who appreciate the

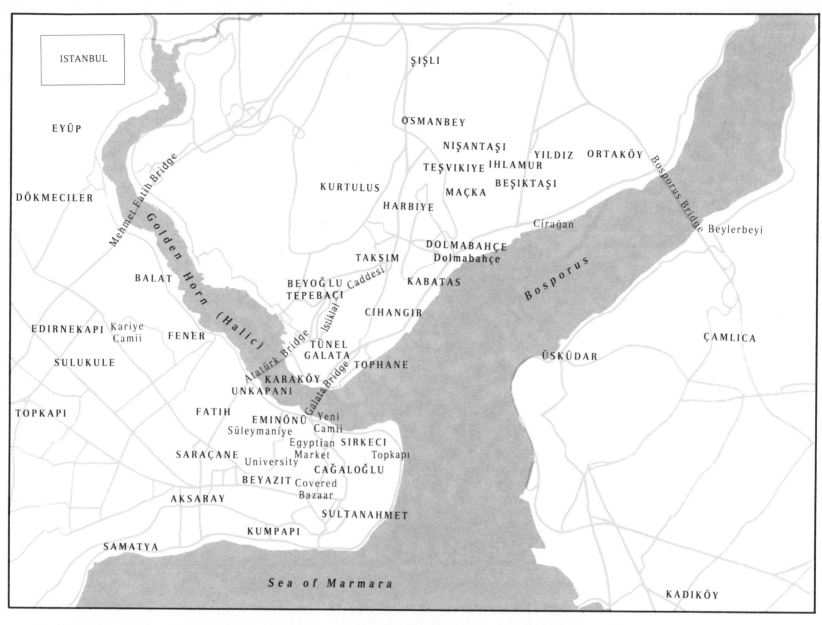

ISTANBUL

EYÜP

DÖKMECILER

ŞIŞLI

OSMANBEY

NIŞANTAŞI

TEŞVIKIYE IHLAMUR YILDIZ ORTAKÖY

Bosporus Bridge

KURTULUŞ MAÇKA BEŞIKTAŞI

HARBIYE

Mehmet Fatih Bridge

Golden Horn (Haliç)

Cirağan

Beylerbeyi

DOLMABAHÇE
Dolmabahçe

BALAT

TAKSIM

BEYOĞLU Caddesi KABATAŞ

TEPEBAŞI

Bosporus

EDIRNEKAPI Kariye
Camii FENER

CIHANGIR

ÇAMLICA

Istiklal Caddesi

SULUKULE

TÜNEL
GALATA

Atatürk Bridge

ÜSKÜDAR

TOPHANE

KARAKÖY

Galata Bridge

TOPKAPI

UNKAPANI

FATIH

EMINÖNÜ Yeni
Camii

Süleymaniye

SARAÇANE

Egyptian SIRKECI
Market Topkapı

University

CAĞALOĞLU

BEYAZIT Covered
Bazaar

AKSARAY

SULTANAHMET

KUMPAPI

SAMATYA

Sea of Marmara

KADIKÖY

establishment's fish, caviar and *blinis*. It also serves very good Turkish meat dishes.

Asitane
Kariye Camii Sokak 18,
EDIRNEKAPI
Tel.: (212) 534 84 14
The seasonal menu is only one of the attractions of this historic restaurant in the Kariye Hotel. There is traditional Turkish music to entertain you as you sample the restaurant's specialities, notably *saksi kebabi*, a spring chicken stew garnished with aubergine purée and *helatiye*, cubes of steamed pudding

made with almonds and pistachio nuts, covered in rose-water syrup.

Beyti
Orman Sokak 8, FLORYA
Tel.: (212) 663 29 90
This restaurant on one of the handsome avenues of Florya is a good choice for a farewell dinner in Istanbul, not only because it serves excellent grilled meats, but also because it is near the airport.

Borsa
Halaskargazi Caddesi, Şair Nigar Sokak 90/1, OSMANBEY
Tel.: (212) 232 42 00

For those who wish to go shopping in the elegant districts of Osmanbey and Nisantasi, this is the perfect place for lunch. The menu consists of traditional dishes which, according to the restaurant's Turkish clientele, taste like home cooking—the highest praise a Turkish restaurant can receive.

Çiçek Paşajı
Istiklal Caddesi, Galatasaray,
BEYOĞLU
(see pp. 222, 223)
The Flower Arcade, once the city's liveliest thoroughfare,

houses a number of restaurants, notably Entellektüel Cavit's (tel.: (212) 244 71 29). They are classic traditional restaurants not to be missed, serving, for example, delicious Turkish hors d'œuvres, *böreks*, or stuffed mussels.

Club 29
Nispetiye Caddesi 29, ETILER
Tel.: (212) 263 54 11 (winter)
Paşabahçe Yolu 24, ÇUBUKLU
Tel.: (216) 322 38 88 (summer)
(see pp. 238, 239)
The sumptuous decor of this combined bar, club and restaurant evokes all the indolence of the

Orient. Here you can lunch by the pool, spend the evening dancing or relax on one of the many divans which nestle in the delightful alcoves. The prices in the restaurant itself are high, but —if certain gourmets are to be believed— it serves the best *köfte* in all Istanbul. If you are coming from the opposite bank of the Bosporus, the restaurant will send a boat to ferry you across.

Darüzziyafe
Sifahane Caddesi 6, Süleymaniye,
BEYAZIT
Tel.: (212) 511 84 14

Located in the heart of the Süleymaniye complex—one of Sinan's masterpieces—this restaurant has an inner courtyard where you can escape from the hubbub of the old town. It used to be the Ottoman equivalent of a workman's café and traditional cooking is still the order of the day: Süleyman soup, lamb kebab, *böreks*, desserts, sorbets, etc. The setting and the atmosphere of this restaurant, however, are more important than the cuisine.

Develi
Balıkpazari, Gümüşyüzük Sokak 7, SAMATYA
Tel.: (212) 585 11 89, 585 43 86
There is such a wealth of restaurants in Istanbul that it is often difficult to know where to go to be sure of eating the best *köfte*. The Develi will not disappoint you. This restaurant, which has been in existence for 80 years, offers Anatolian cuisine with a wide choice of kebabs.

Divan
Divan Hotel,
Cumhuriyet Caddesi 2, ŞİŞLİ
Tel.: (212) 231 41 00
Long after more fashionable restaurants have disappeared, the Divan will doubtless still be serving its Turkish and Continental specialities to gourmets. The restaurant is quiet, with an elegant, refined decor and perfect service.

Ece
Tramvay Caddesi 104,
Kuruçesme,
ARNAVUTKÖY
Tel.: (212) 265 96 00
This lively restaurant, which is very popular with younger Turks, is spread over three floors. According to your appetite, you can opt for the set menu or else choose your own *à la carte*. The vegetable dishes, and in particular beans, are a house speciality.

Façyo
Kireçburnu Caddesi 13, TARABYA
Tel.: (212) 262 00 24
(see p. 228)
This restaurant serves the best fish in the area, but it is also a pleasant place to spend the evening after exploring this one-time fishing village, now famous for its nightlife and its ice cream.

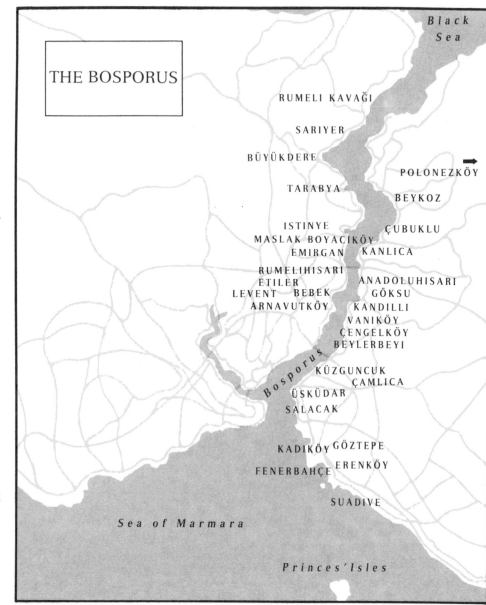

THE BOSPORUS

Black Sea

RUMELI KAVAĞI
SARIYER
BÜYÜKDERE
TARABYA
POLONEZKÖY
BEYKOZ
ISTINYE
MASLAK BOYACIKÖY
EMIRGAN
ÇUBUKLU
KANLICA
RUMELIHISARI
ETILER
ANADOLUHISARI
LEVENT BEBEK
GÖKSU
ARNAVUTKÖY
KANDILLI
VANIKÖY
ÇENGELKÖY
BEYLERBEYI
KÜZGUNCUK
ÇAMLICA
ÜSKÜDAR
SALACAK
KADIKÖY GÖZTEPE
ERENKÖY
FENERBAHÇE
SUADIVE
Bosporus
Sea of Marmara
Princes' Isles

Hacı Baba
Istiklal Caddesi 49, BEYOĞLU
Tel.: (212) 244 18 86
A word of warning about this restaurant: the zealous *maître d'hôtel* will show you so many Turkish hors d'œuvres, kebabs, stews and desserts, and the choice will be so hard, that you will probably end up ordering far more than you can eat.

Hasan Balıkçılar Lokantası
Yat Limanı, Rıhtım Sokak 8, YEŞİLKÖY
Tel.: (212) 573 83 00
This noisy, expensive restaurant

near the airport is renowned for its extraordinary fish dishes, its rudimentary comfort and its dessert of quinces and cream.

Hasır (Asir)
Kalyoncukulluk Caddesi 94/1, BEYOĞLU
Tel.: (212) 250 05 57
This luxurious restaurant offers tasty hors d'œuvres and elaborate meat dishes. One of the house specialities is *keskek kebab*, which is a lamb purée with butter and cinnamon. The service is excellent and you will undoubtedly enjoy the view over the gardens and the Bosporus.

Hasır
Beykoz Korusu, BEYKOZ
Tel.: (216) 322 29 01
On the Asian bank of the Bosporus, this restaurant is surrounded by gardens. The waiters are attentive and the menu includes memorable meat dishes and other Turkish specialities, as well as delicious sweets. It is worth visiting during Ramadan for the special menus.

Kadife Chalet
Kadife Sokak, Bahariye, KADIKÖY
Tel.: (216) 347 85 96

This Ottoman-style restaurant is located in a hundred-year-old wooden house. Here you have a choice of various specialities from different countries: the house salad, *pirojki*, crêpes, fresh tarts, etc.

Kallavi
Istiklal Caddesi,
Kallavi Sokak 20,
BEYOĞLU
Tel.: (212) 251 10 10
If you dine at this taverna on a Wednesday or a Saturday, you can sample its tasty hors d'œuvres and delicious kebabs.

Kamil
Gümüşsuyu Yolu 9/1,
BEYKOZ
Tel.: (216) 331 05 94
This is a rather shabby restaurant, but that is part of its charm. It has a marvellous view and its fish dishes are delicious.

Kanaat
Selmanipak Caddesi 25,
ÜSKÜDAR
Tel.: (216) 333 37 91
This is the place for gourmets on a tight budget: for the last 60 years no-one has been able to discover the secret of how this restaurant manages to serve authentic Turkish dishes at more than reasonable prices. But beware: the food tends to be rather rich.

Kathisma
Yeni Akbıyık Caddesi 26,
SULTANAHMET
Tel.: (212) 518 97 10
You will be charmed by the pleasant atmosphere of this restaurant which is spread over four floors. It serves good Turkish and foreign dishes at reasonable prices.

Kazan
Mövenpick Hotel, Büyükdere Caddesi 49, MASLAK
Tel.: (212) 285 09 00
The Turkish restaurants in the Mövenpick Hotel are discreetly elegant and have a buffet service offering a rich variety of delicious hors-d'œuvres, copious enough to form a complete meal in themselves.

Konyalı
SULTANAHMET
Tel.: (212) 513 96 97
Istanbulites like to eat at the marble counter of this restaurant in Topkapı Palace. The delicious

böreks and excellent *köfte* are particularly popular. The view would have delighted the sultan.

Körfez
Körfez Caddesi 78, KANLIKA
Tel.: (216) 332 01 08
Bass cooked in a salt loaf and tasty hors d'œuvres are the specialities of this fish restaurant on the peaceful Asian shore of the Bosporus. In spring and summer clients on the European shore are collected at Rumeli Hisar by the restaurant's boat and are served a delicious cocktail on board.

Kumkapı
There are about 50 restaurants in this fishing port on the Marmara shore. Among the narrow pedestrian streets there is a taverna on every corner, all of them specializing in fish dishes. Try **Cemal** or **Evren**, or pick one out at random.

Küçük Hüdadad Lokantası
Sapçı Han,
Kömür Bekir Sokak 2/4,
EMINÖNÜ
This traditional restaurant, frequented by local shopkeepers and stallholders, will give you an idea of what Turks eat at home. Do not search for a sign because it does not have one. It is situated in the Sapçi Han, opposite Yeni Camii. The owner will make marvellous soups for you, as well as delicious *dolmas* (stuffed vegetables), stews and desserts.

Inci
Salacak Sahil Yolu 1, ÜSKÜDAR
Tel.: (216) 310 69 98
You will certainly be enchanted by the view of the old city and the Bosporus from this new restaurant on the Asian bank as you sample its delicious Turkish hors d'œuvres or wonderful fish dishes.

Leonardo Restaurant
Polonezköy 32,
BEYKOZ
Tel.: (216) 432 30 82
A dependable restaurant in this charming village some 40 kilometres from Istanbul. It serves buffet lunches on weekends and has a very pleasant atmosphere.

Liman Lokantası
Above the ferry waiting room,
KARAKÖY
Tel.: (212) 244 10 33
Many businessmen come here during their lunch hour to escape

the hubbub of Karaköy, with its bustling shopping and business district. The restaurant serves unforgettable seafood and has a view of the quay and the ferries that ply the blue waters of the Golden Horn.

Mey
Rumelihisari Caddesi Bebekli Apt. 122, BEBEK
Tel.: (212) 265 25 99
The principal speciality of this restaurant, an offshoot of the celebrated **Türkbükü** in Bodrum, is fish. The proprietor himself decides on the modestly priced menu. There are few tables and the dishes are cooked according to the number of clients expected, so it is essential to reserve.

Ortaköy
On the Bosporus, north of
BEŞIKTAŞ
In the restaurants of Ortaköy, a picturesque waterside quarter, the food does not perhaps quite reach the standard of the setting—you are as likely to find Mexican food here as Turkish. **Bodrum**, **A la Turka**, **Gulet Çinaralti** and **Ziya**, all of which serve Turkish and international dishes, are among the best restaurants here. Beware of crowds on Sundays.

Pandeli
Egyptian Market (Mısır Çarşısı),
EMINÖNÜ
Tel.: (212) 527 39 09
(see p. 234)
This restaurant, which serves

absolutely delicious food, is in the Egyptian Market. The aubergine *börek* is wonderful and is worth asking for instead of the hors d'œuvres that are usually served as a matter of course.

Park Samdan
Mim Kemal Öke Caddesi 18/1,
NIŞANTAŞI
Tel.: (212) 240 83 68

Etiler Samdan
Nispetiye Caddesi 30, ETILER
Tel.: (212) 263 48 98
These two restaurants belonging to an important Turkish family are among the most fashionable in Istanbul. The Etiler restaurant serves Turko-French cuisine and has an after-dinner discotheque. The Park Samdan is ideally placed for those who wish to shop in the area.

Refik
Sofyalı Sokak 10-12, TÜNEL
Tel.: (212) 243 28 34
The proprietor of this unpretentious Turkish restaurant, in which the accent is placed on Black Sea specialities, loves to chat with his customers, whatever their language. His Turkish patrons have a weakness for his stuffed cabbage.

Resat Paşa Konaği
Bağlarbaşi Caddesi 34/1,
ERENKÖY
Tel.: (216) 361 34 11
In this carefully restored villa, Turkish cookery and *nouvelle cuisine* have been skilfully

blended. Its small, intimate rooms make it ideal for a hearty Sunday brunch.

Revan
Sheraton Hotel, TAKSIM
Tel.: (212) 231 21 21
The restaurant is on the 23rd floor of the hotel and has a panoramic view over the city. You might start with a *puf börek*, or, if you prefer soup, the nuptial soup *düğün çorbasi*, in which the main ingredient is yoghurt. Whatever you choose you will not be disappointed, for the Revan is one of the best restaurants in Istanbul.

'S' Restaurant
Vezirköşkü Sokak 2, BEBEK
Tel.: (212) 263 83 26
Connoisseurs will tell you that this is the *nec plus ultra*, and they will not be wrong. *Nouvelle cuisine*-style Turkish delights await you in this expensive restaurant, where candlelight and wainscotting create a refined atmosphere and evening dress is required.

Sans
Hacı Adil Sokak 1, LEVENT
Tel.: (212) 281 07 07
Engravings of plants and tapestry designs decorate the walls of Sans, which means 'luck' (a key element of Turkish tradition). If you are in luck, you will be given a table near the parrot, who will be delighted to make conversation while you sample the Turkish and European specialities.

Sarniç
Soğukçeşme Sokak,
SULTANAHMET
Tel.: (212) 512 42 91
The dishes served in this restaurant close to the Ayasofya Hotel are nothing special, but the setting—an underground Roman cistern—is unforgettable.

Sultanahmet Köfteçisi
Divanyolu Caddesi 12A,
SULTANAHMET
Tel.: (212) 513 14 38
A modest chain of restaurants which has been well known for its *köfte* for 90 years. No alcohol.

Süreyya
Istinye Caddesi 26, ISTINYE
Tel.: (212) 277 58 86
This restaurant offers the best of eastern-western cooking. The menu owes its originality to the owner of the restaurant, who is of Russian descent. It includes bortsch, chicken Kiev and beef stroganoff. A real treat! Booking is essential.

Susam Restaurant
Susam Sokak 6, CIHANGIR
Tel.: (212) 251 59 35
A smart restaurant and bar in an old district which has extensive grounds and a good view of Seraglio Point. It is open for lunch and dinner and is especially pleasant in summer. Reservations essential.

Tuğra
Çirağan, BEŞIKTAŞ
Tel.: (212) 258 33 77
You cannot fail to notice the golden *tuğra* (sultan's calligraphic monogram), which is the pride and joy of the owner, who will serve you dishes of equally fine quality. The menu features complex yet extremely refined Ottoman dishes. Here in the elegant setting of the Çiragan Hotel, let yourself be tempted by a hot hors d'œuvre such as an aubergine *börek* or a tiny swordfish kebab.

Urcan
Orta Ceşme Caddesi 2/1, SARIYER
Tel.: (212) 242 03 67
Everybody has heard of Urcan and its large rooms decorated with fishing nets, and its fish, attractively displayed at the entrance, that look as though they have just come out of the water. It is as popular as ever and well worth the trip up the Bosporus.

Yakup 2

Asmalı Mescit Sokak 35-37,
TÜNEL
Tel.: (212) 249 29 25
Join the Turkish artists, journalists and intellectuals who gather in this authentic, noisy and unpretentious *meyhane*.

Yekta

Valikonaği Caddesi 39/1,
NIŞANTAŞI
Tel.: (212) 248 11 83
The menu at Yekta is not limited to Turkish dishes, but the proprietor, Selim Isatan, takes great care over the flavour and colour of the food.

Yirmidokuz (29) Ulus

Ulus Parki, ULUS
Tel.: (212) 265 61 81, 265 61 98
The latest restaurant and bar opened by Istanbul's top restaurateurs, Metin and Zeynep Fadıllıoğlu. It offers an amazing view of the Bosporus which takes in both bridges. The elegant interior evokes a nomad tent. The menu offers excellent Turkish and Continental cuisine and its French dishes are prepared by a French chef. Reservations essential.

Ziya

Mim Kemal Öke Caddesi 21/1,
NIŞANTAŞI
Tel.: (212) 225 46 65
Whatever the time of day, Ziya is full of Istanbul businessmen and foreigners who have come for a meal or simply a drink. There are no unpleasant surprises and, with a bit of luck, you might even be able to eat on the terrace.

Ziya

Muallim Naci Caddesi 109/1,
ORTAKÖY
Tel.: (212) 261 60 05
You will enjoy the view from this restaurant situated in the shadow of the Bosporus Bridge. In summer you can eat outside on the terrace.

CAFÉS

Anadolu Kavagi Café

Yoros Fortress, ANADOLU KAVAGI
This café inside the walls of the Genovese fortress of Yoros, with its tables set out beneath a trellis, is a good place to stop for some tea or a light meal accompanied by vegetables from the café's garden. There is a beautiful view of the Bosporus extending as far as the Black Sea.

Pera Café

Istiklal Caddesi, Hava Sokak
17/2, BEYOĞLU
Tel.: (212) 251 24 35
This popular café in Beyoğlu is a good place for coffee, as well as for lunch or dinner. Let yourself be tempted by the delicious crepes served with home-made syrup.

Café de Pera

(Pera Palas Hotel)
Mesrutiyet Caddesi, TEPEBAŞI
Tel.: (212) 251 45 60
This legendary café in the famous century-old Pera Palas Hotel has a turn-of-the-century decor and delicious cakes which are served to the strains of classical music. The owners have opened a second café in Bebek: Insirah Yokusu, Bebek Çikmazi Sokak 1, tel.: (212) 257 10 53.

Café Kaktüs

Istiklal Caddesi, Imam Adnan
Sokak 4, BEYOĞLU
Tel.: (212) 249 59 79
A softly lit and elegant bistro specializing in light but delicious European food. Excellent cheesecake and piped classical music and jazz.

Keyif Café

Mim Kemal Öke Caddesi 4/1,
NIŞANTAŞI
Tel.: (212) 225 20 19
A popular new café frequented by the city's most fashion-conscious inhabitants during the day. It offers breakfast and light lunches and dinners. Open until 10 p.m.

Café Lebon

Istiklal Caddesi 463, BEYOĞLU
Tel.: (212) 252 98 52
During the *belle époch* Istanbulites used to come to this café for tea or coffee. Although recently restored and incorporated into the Richmond Hotel, Café Lebon has retained its charm. As well as lunch and dinner, it serves delicious cakes.

Ibrahim Paşa's Palace Café

At Meydanı 46, SULTANAHMET
Tel.: (212) 518 13 85
When the paşa decided to move into this palace, it may have been because of the magnificent views over the Bosporus from the upper floor. Maybe he used to drink his coffee at the very spot where the museum's small round café tables stand today. This place provides a welcome escape from the crowds of Sultanahmet, Istanbul's main tourist area.

Archaeological Museum Café

SULTANAHMET
Tel.: (212) 520 77 40
(see pp. 40, 228)
This open-air café is located in the grounds of the museum, next to the Çinili Kösk. The surrounding fragments of marble statues will take you back in time to antiquity.

Çamlıca Café

Sefa Tepesi, ÇAMLIKA
Tel.: (216) 329 81 91
(see pp. 226, 227)
If the weather is bright, do not hesitate to spend an entire

afternoon in the gardens of this café: from the top of the promontory one can see the whole of the city. In winter, you can sit in front of the fire.

Çorlulu Ali Paşa Café

BEYAZIT
(see pp. 58, 225)
The general to whom the mosque and the café owe their name was Ahmet III's Grand Vizier. It is a pleasant place for a rest after a visit to the mosque complex and you can also experiment with smoking a hookah.

Emirgan Park

Tel.: (212) 227 66 82
The Yellow Kiosk Café, ideal for lunch or brunch every day of the week, is housed in an elegant wooden building in the delightful historic Emirgan Park. In the same park, the charming Beyaz Kösk Restaurant is another good place to eat a light meal.

Gramofon

Tünel Meydanı 5,
Tünel, BEYOĞLU
Tel.: (212) 293 07 86
In these tearooms in the ravishing little nineteenth-century square by the Tünel, you can linger over your tea or coffee to the sound of gentle music and the clicking of the old red trams.

Kariye Café

Edirnekapi Son Durak, Kariye
Camii Sokak, EDIRNEKAPI
Tel.: (212) 534 84 14

The white and lilac walls of this restored café (and the hotel of the same name), in the same square as the Kariye Mosque, will certainly catch your eye. It is a pleasant spot for coffee after you have seen the remarkable mosaics.

Palazzo

Maçka Caddesi 35,
TEŞVIKIYE
Tel.: (212) 232 04 51
This fashionable café in the old Maçka Palace would be as much at home in Bologna or Florence, with its young clientele and tasty cappuccino—a speciality, incidentally, that is hard to find in Turkey. You can enjoy a good sandwich or salad before your coffee or eat home-made cake with it.

Pierre Loti

EYÜP
Tel.: (212) 581 26 96
A walk to this little café in the historic Eyüp quarter should be a must for every visitor to Istanbul. Pierre Loti often used to come here, hence its name. It can be reached by crossing the romantic cemetery and its terrace offers a beautiful view over the Golden Horn.

Pub Divan Elmadag

Cumhuriyet Caddesi 2, Elmadag,
ŞIŞLI (part of the Divan Hotel)
Tel.: (212) 231 41 00

Pub Divan Erenköy

Bagdat Caddesi 361, ERENKÖY
Tel.: (216) 355 16 40
In the Divan Hotel's Pub café you will rub shoulders with Istanbul high society, who come here to enjoy a *döner kebab* or lighter dishes, made, for example, with chicken breast. Both places also have delicious cakes and sweets, which can be eaten on the spot or taken away.

Romantika

In Fenerbahçe Park
FENER
Tel.: (216) 347 29 80
This tearoom is in a Victorian-style belvedere which, contrary to what one might think, is only 20 years old. Here, on the Fenerbahçe peninsula, in the heart of this charming little park, you can eat cakes accompanied by a hot drink (real *sahlep* in winter), surrounded by tropical plants and an aviary which create a most pleasant atmosphere.

Sark Kahvesi

Tel.: (212) 512 11 44
(see p. 64)
This oriental café, inside the Covered Bazaar, is practically an institution.

Vakko

Istiklal Caddesi 123-125,
BEYOĞLU
Tel.: (212) 251 40 92
No visit to the modern city would be complete without at least an hour spent at the café in Vakko, the Turkish fashion department store. Over a cup of tea and a slice of chocolate cake you will discover that Vakko is much more than that. It is in fact a very popular café and an art gallery.

Yıldız Park

BEŞIKTAŞ
Malta Köskü
Tel.: (212) 260 04 54
Çadir Köskü
Tel.: (212) 260 07 09
Pembe Köskü
In this impressive park there are three delightful places to have tea. Çadir, Malta, and Pembe Kösks are all pavilions built which were by the Ottomans in the last century and renovated by the Turkish Touring and Automobile Club under its inspired director, Çelik Gülersoy.

Zanzibar Café

Teşvikiye Caddesi 60, Reasürans Çarşısı, TEŞVIKIYE
Tel.: (212) 233 80 46
A new place already popular with young people, who like its piped African and New Age music and French snacks. Closed Sundays.

Zencefil Café and Shop

Kurabiye Sokak 3, BEYOĞLU
Tel.: (212) 244 40 82
A cosy and charming café serving a limited but delicious menu that changes every day and includes specialities from different countries, wonderful home-made breads, fruit teas and wine. Popular with intellectuals. Also sells local herbs, jams and spices. Closed Mondays.

BARS

Bebek Bar

Cevdet Paşa Caddesi 15, BEBEK
Tel.: (212) 263 30 00
In this fashionable bar you will be able to admire the scenery on the opposite bank of the Bosporus while sampling the house cocktail made of gin, vodka, brandy, lemon juice, orange juice, and rose liqueur.

Cabaret Cine

Yeşilpinar Sokak 2,
ARNAVUTKÖY
Tel.: (212) 257 74 38
If you want to explore the village of Arnavutköy with its handsome wooden houses, why not begin by drinking a cocktail in this lively bar, with its extraordinary view?

Memo

Salhane Sokak 10/2, ORTAKÖY
Tel.: (212) 261 83 04
This large bar-cum-restaurant close to the Bosporus Bridge attracts a distinguished clientele. Live music and discotheque in the evening.

Orient Express Bar

Pera Palas Hotel, TEPEBAŞI
Tel.: (212) 251 45 60
They will tell you here that Garbo used to come surrounded by a whole court of admirers, that Hemingway could not resist the pleasure of a *raki*, and that Graham Greene used to write at one of the little tables with pretty lamps. In this bar, which has succeeded in preserving its charm and sacrificed nothing to progress, you have a date with the past.

Ortaköy

On the Bosporus, north of
BEŞIKTAŞ
Ortaköy is a district where it is pleasant to spend an evening going from one bar to another. The views of the Bosporus and the crowds of trendy people are as enjoyable as the music in the bars.

Try the Christina, the Merhaba, the Prince or the Rubber. They are all less crowded on weekdays.

Papillon

Selcuklar Sokak 16,
Beşinci Yil Çarşısı 21-3,
ETILER
Tel.: (212) 257 39 46
(see pp. 236, 237)
This discotheque, frequented by young people, was designed by Hakan Ezer.

Süleyman Nazif

Valikonagi Caddesi 39,
NIŞANTAŞI
Tel.: (212) 225 22 43
A three-roomed flat decorated in the Ottoman style forms the setting for this nightspot. Ensconced in one of the comfortable armchairs in one of the bars, you will appreciate the quality of the service and the tasty morsels provided, though you may be surprised, or even irritated, by the images on the television screens around you.

Taxim

Nizamiye Caddesi 12-16,
TAKSIM
Tel.: (212) 256 44 31
(see p. 237)
Nigel Coates, the *enfant terrible* of British architecture, displayed all his talent and originality in his design for this discotheque in the heart of the city. It is open on Fridays and Saturdays and is coupled with a restaurant that is open all week.

Zihni

Brouz Sokak 1/B, MAÇKA
Tel.: (212) 246 90 43
The decor of Zihni, a mixture of strangely uncoordinated elements, is startling. Its clientele of young professional people is less so. This café closes relatively early.

SWEETS, CAKES AND ICES

Bebek Badem Ezmesi

Cevdet Paşa Caddesi 238/1,
BEBEK
Tel.: (212) 232 04 51
This very elegant little shop has been selling its wonderful almond and pistachio marzipan for the last 90 years. It is probably the best cake shop in the city.

Divan

Divan Hotel, ŞIŞLI
Tel.: (212) 231 41 00
Bagdat Caddesi, ERENKÖY
Tel.: (216) 355 16 40
This is truly the king of sweet shops. A visit is a must for those who wish to sample the best Turkish delight, cakes and ice creams in all Istanbul.

Güllüoglu

Mısır Çarşısı 88,
EMINÖNÜ
Tel. (212) 528 51 81
This family establishment makes some of the best pistachio *baklavas* in the city. The family owns another shop opposite the ferry passenger lounge in Karaköy (tel.: (212) 244 45 67).

Hacı Bekir

Istiklal Caddesi 124/2, BEYOĞLU
Tel.: (212) 245 13 75
Before going to the cinema or after a dinner in the old quarter of Pera, stop off at this cake shop. It is frequented by Turks, who always demand the best when it comes to *yas pasta*, *kuru pasta*, or Turkish delight flavoured with rose-water, nuts or lemon. The owners run a second shop near Sirkeci Station (tel.: (212) 244 28 04).

Hacıbozanoğullarıı

Nispetiye Caddesi 42/6, ETILER
Tel.: (212) 263 38 72
This cake shop is an obligatory stop for Turks on their way to and from work, whether it be to buy a cake to replace breakfast or *baklava* for the evening meal. There are 50 specialities to choose from. There are nine Hacibozanogullarii cake shops throughout the city.

Inci

Istiklal Caddesi 124/1, BEYOĞLU
Tel.: (212) 243 24 12
Rattling trams and ambling passers-by form the backdrop to this cake shop that has been serving profiteroles since 1944 and is a veritable landmark in Istiklal Caddesi.

Pera Patisserie

Pera Palas Hotel, TEPEBAŞI
Tel.: (212) 251 45 60
Endless fresh coffee, mouthwatering cakes and an art nouveau decor await you in this delightful tearoom.

Üç-Yıldız

Duduodalari Sokak 15,
BEYOĞLU
Tel.: (212) 244 81 70
(see pp. 232-33)
Here in the heart of Galatasaray Market, you will find the best *halvah* and the freshest Turkish delight, made in the rooms above the shop. The proprietor will be happy to tell you the story behind the striking jam jars that decorate his shop.

FOOD SHOPS

Asrı Turşucu

Agahamam Caddesi 29/A,
CIHANGIR
Tel.: (212) 251 48 76
This shop, which has been in existence for 70 years, sells all sorts of cereals, fruit and pickled vegetables.

Konyalı

Emlak Kredi Çarşısı, SİRKECİ
Tel.: (212) 268 26 54
This shop, also a cafeteria, is located in front of the Sirkeci Station. It offers cooked dishes, cakes and traditional milk products.

Kurukahveci Mehmet Efendi

Mısır Çarşısı, EMİNÖNÜ
Tel.: (212) 511 42 62
(see p. 68)
Situated in the heart of the Egyptian Market, this is one of Istanbul's institutions. Shoppers can find Turkish coffee here, as well as *sahlep* prepackaged in attractive sachets.

Sütis

TAKSİM
Tel.: (212) 243 72 04
Teşvikiye Caddesi 137/A,
NİŞANTAŞI
Tel.: (212) 248 35 07
EMİRGAN
Tel.: (212) 277 63 73
Turkey's little-known dairy produce is truly delicious. Where dairy produce from other countries can taste sugary, here it is subtly sweetened and traditionally garnished with nuts and dried fruits.

Sütte

Balıkpazarı, Duduodalar Sokak 21, Galatasaray, BEYOĞLU
Tel.: (212) 244 07 54,
(212) 293 92 92
Nispetiye Caddesi, Çamlic Sokak 2,
ETİLER
Tel.: (212) 263 66 56
The Polish owners of this delicatessen, the best in the city, were the first people to sell pork in Istanbul.
Turkish students have a weakness for their sandwiches, while the elegant clientele fill their picnic baskets with the shop's choicer products.

Tiryaki

Şair Nigar Sokak 1, NİŞANTAŞI
Tel.: (212) 240 55 71
This delightful shop specializes in coffee beans, teas, dried fruit and nuts.

Vefa Bozacısı

Atatürk Bulvarı 146/B, AKSARAY
Tel.: (212) 527 66 08
The drink made from fermented millet, *boza*, has been a house speciality since 1876.
You will finish by liking this very unusual beverage.

HAMAMS

Cağaloğlu Hamami

Prof. Kazim Gürkan Caddesi 34,
CAĞALOĞLU
Tel.: (212) 522 24 24
(see pp. 18, 19, 195, 205, 208)
The marble rooms of this *hamam* are almost 300 years old. Past visitors include King Edward VIII, Franz Liszt, Florence Nightingale and Rudolf Nureyev. There are separate rooms for men and women, as well as mixed rooms.

Çemberlitaş Hamamı

Vezirhan Caddesi 8,
ÇEMBERLİTAŞ
Tel.: (212) 522 79 74
This white stone *hamam* was built 450 years ago and designed by Mimar Sinan. It is not far from the Covered Bazaar.

Galatasaray Hamamı

Turuncubasi Sokak, BEYOĞLU
Tel.: (212) 249 43 42
In the heart of Beyoğlu, this is one of the more popular *hamams* with Istanbulites.

Kiliç Ali Paşa Hamamı

Kemeraltı Caddesi, TOPHANE
Tel.: (212) 244 70 37
(see pp. 206, 207)
Named after an admiral who met the Spanish author Cervantes in North Africa and freed him from captivity. Sinan's design for this *hamam* influenced the architecture of Haghia Sophia.

Küçük Mustafa Paşa Hamamı

Küçük Mustafa Paşa Sokak,
FENER
TEL.: (212) 589 11 46
(see pp. 196, 197, 198, 200, 201)
This is one of the oldest, largest and finest *hamams* still in operation. It is situated in one of the old quarters by the Golden Horn which are not often explored by the tourist.

Ortaköy Hamamı

Muallim Naci Caddesi 79,
ORTAKÖY
Tel.: (212) 259 35 84
(see p. 199)
Don't be put off by the ordinary appearance of this *hamam*, which dates from 1544. The interior, which has been restored, is worthy of the paşa who had it built.

MARKETS

Ak Merkez

ETİLER
A plush, modern shopping mall, which houses the city's best fashion boutiques, as well as fast-food places, small cinemas and a large food market.

Balıkpazarı (Fish Market)

Galatasaray,
BEYOĞLU
You will find a little of everything in this market, with its fascinating and beautifully presented stalls and its extraordinary variety of fish. One of the market's passages leads directly onto the Çiçek Pasajı.

Beşiktaş Pazarı

BEŞİKTAŞ
In this market, one of the largest open-air markets in Istanbul, one can find everything from food to gardening tools. The prices are reasonable, but do not hesitate to bargain if your Turkish is up to it.

Covered Bazaar (Kapalı Çarşı)

BEYAZIT (see pp. 64-65)
The most fertile imagination cannot begin to conceive of what this market is like. Its sheer size and the maze of arcades will totally confuse you. In the past it sold only gold, but nowadays you can find a multitude of different treasures there.

Egyptian Market (Mısır Çarşısı)

EMİNÖNÜ (see p. 69)
The Egyptian Market, often known as the Spice Bazaar, is the place for all sorts of spices of every colour, but it also sells an exotic selection of plants, baskets and birds. Try and avoid this market on weekends and on public holidays.

Ortaköy Pazarı

ORTAKÖY
This is a Sunday crafts market held in the narrow streets around the mosque in Ortaköy.

Salı Pazarı

KADIKÖY
This is where Istanbulites go to buy everything they need, from food to flowers, toys to plastic crockery. Said to be the largest in the whole of Turkey, this market is fascinating and always crowded.

It takes place on Tuesdays in the streets of Kadiköy on the Asian bank of the Bosporus.

JEWELLERS

Artisan

Şakayık Sokak 54/1, NİŞANTAŞI
Tel.: (212) 247 90 81
This shop sells some extraordinary antique and handmade jewellery.

Cendereci

Teşvikiye Caddesi 125, TEŞVİKİYE
Tel.: (212) 247 98 33
Jeweller Herbert Cendereci designs pieces based on Roman jewellery from the fifth century BC. He comes from a Caucasian Turkish family which has been in the jewellery business for ten years. He owns another shop in the Covered Bazaar at Sira Odlar Hanı 24.

Franguli

Istiklal Caddesi, near Galatasaray, BEYOĞLU
Tel.: (212) 244 56 70
The best jewellers in town are traditionally of Armenian origin and this one is no exception. Mr Vincent, the owner of the shop, is considered to be an expert. Located on Istiklal Caddesi, near the Galata quarter, the shop has been selling traditional Turkish jewellery in gold and precious stones since 1950.

Gönul Paksoy

Atiye Sokak 6/A, TEŞVİKİYE
Tel.: (212) 261 90 81
There are two shops of this name and the more recent one is up the street at number 1. They both sell unusual jewellery (unique pieces) and clothes dyed with natural dyes, along with small rugs and kilims. The proprietor, who is a chemistry graduate, has developed new methods in dyeing.

Lapis

Nuruosmaniye Caddesi 75-77,
CAĞALOĞLU
Tel.: (212) 511 05 50
Lapis is one of the biggest shops selling carpets, leather goods and jewellery.

Leon Camic

Kapalı Çarşı
Tel.: (212) 522 30 56
Situated in the Covered Bazaar, this is one of the oldest jewellery shops in the city. The prices are relatively high, but justifiably so. Even if you are not going to buy anything, at least go and admire this stunning collection.

Neslihan Simavi—Feride Cansever
Kapalı Çarşı
Tel.: (212) 519 23 29
This talented designer makes all sorts of pieces, including traditional Turkish cups and bowls in silver. If you wish to make a special order, you will have to go to Neslihan's workshop. Telephone for an appointment.

Urart
Abdi Ipekçi Caddesi 18/1, Nişantaşı
Tel.: (212) 246 71 94
This shop and art gallery (a favourite among Istanbul connoisseurs) sells designer jewellery that is inspired by, or copied from, Hittite, Graeco-Roman or Ottoman pieces.

V-22
Teşvikiye Caddesi, TEŞVIKIYE
Tel.: (212) 231 57 42
This jeweller has an impressive collection of quality Turkish jewellery, including silver set with semi-precious stones.

BOOKS

Çelik Gülersoy Library
Soğukçesme Sokak, SULTANAHMET
Tel.: (212) 512 57 30
An impressive collection of books on Istanbul.

Eren
Sofyali Sokak 34, Tünel, BEYOĞLU
Tel.: (212) 251 28 58
This bookshop has a special place in the hearts of foreigners living in Istanbul: it is one of the rare bookshops in which you will find art and history books (some of them old) in English, French, German and Turkish. There is a branch in the second-hand book market, Sahaflar Çarşışı (tel. (212) 522 85 31).

Haset Kitabevi
Istiklal Caddesi 469, BEYOĞLU
Tel.: (212) 249 10 06
This bookshop has a good selection of books in English, French and German.

Levant
Tünel Meydani 8, Tünel, BEYOĞLU
Tel.: (212) 293 63 33
You will find engravings, postcards, maps and second-hand books here.

Pera Bookshop
Galip Dede Sokak 22, Tünel, BEYOĞLU
Tel.: (212) 245 49 98
This bookshop has been specializing in old books for over 80 years. It has a wide selection of books in foreign languages, including Greek, Armenian and Arabic, as well as in Turkish. It also has a very good section on the history of Istanbul, including books by foreign authors.

Rare Book Market
Booksellers are grouped in the Sahaflar Çarşısı, in the old town (see p. 67), although this market is not as interesting as it used to be. There are some good dealers in Aslihan Passage, in Galatasary, and others in the Akmar alley in Kadiköy, not far from the ferry landing stage.

Women's Library
FENER
Tel.: (212) 523 74 00
The historic building in the old quarter of Fener by the Golden Horn which houses this library will be of more interest to the visitor than its contents.

ANTIQUE SHOPS

Abdül Antiques
Kalıpçı Sokak 119/2 TEŞVIKIYE
Tel.: (212) 231 74 79
This is a good place for carpets, silverware, furniture, china, calligraphic inscriptions and paintings.

Chalabi Antiques
Mim Kemal Öke Caddesi 17, NIŞANTAŞI
Tel.: (212) 225 01 85
This shop sells Ottoman and European furniture as well as pottery and paintings.

Çukurcuma Antique Market
Çukurcuma, CIHANGIR
This delightful antique market in the little streets surrounding Firuzaga Mosque in Cihangir has a number of interesting dealers, notably the following:

Alfa Gallery
Hacioğlu Sokak 1, Çukurcuma
Tel.: (212) 251 16 72
This shop run by Marianna Yerasimo sells a variety of antiques, including maps, engravings, paintings and books in various European languages.

Çatma Antik
Çukurcuma Camii Sokak 5, Çukurcuma
Tel.: (212) 252 44 90
The charming owner of this shop is particularly fond of nineteenth-century Tokat jugs in yellow or plain green. She also sells antique gold-embroidered *hamam* towels.

Leyla Seyhanlı
Altıpatlar Sokak 10-30,
Tel.: (212) 243 74 10
You will admire the beautiful clothes—especially the old traditional costumes—sold in this shop, as well as the fine Ottoman and European fabrics.

Asli Günşiray
Firuzaga Mahallesi, Çukurcuma Caddesi 74,
Tel.: (212) 252 59 86
The owner of this shop is famous for having started a new fashion: he rescues the old carved wooden doors from Anatolian houses and converts them into table-tops or wall hangings.

Yağmur Kayabek
Altıpatlar Sokak 8,
Tel.: (212) 244 88 89
Yagmur, the son of a well-known antique dealer, sells handsome examples of Ottoman calligraphy and other Islamic artefacts.

Maison de l'Authentique
Firuzaga Mahallesi, Çukurcuma Caddesi 48/50,
Tel.: (212) 252 79 23
In this well-organized shop covering an area of 300 square metres you will find furniture, furnishings and fabrics. One of the owners, Esra Onat, is a painter and her artistic touches are clearly visible in the decor of the shop's café.

Yaman Mursaloğlu
Faikpasa Caddesi 41, Çukurcuma,
Tel.: (212) 251 95 87
(see p. 172)
This specialist in Ottoman art divides his time between London and Istanbul.

Horhor Flea Market
Kirk Tulunba Sokak 13/22
AKSARAY
This market near the Aqueduct

of Valens, is comparable to Mecidiyeköy antique market both in size and prices (do not expect to get a reduction). The market will, however, give you a good idea of the incredible variety of Ottoman artefacts available in Istanbul.

Kemal Değer
Mevlanakapı Caddesi 4, TOPKAPI
You might have some difficulty in finding this shop, which is inside the walls of the old acropolis, but, whatever you do, don't be discouraged.

Kuledibi Flea Market
GALATA
People may tell you that this second-hand furniture market has seen better days and that it has lost its character, but don't let that stop you from paying it a quick visit, if only to compare prices. From Galata Tower, you walk behind the square and then turn right down the street leading to Sishane.

Mecidiyeköy Antikacilar Çarşısı (Antique Market)
Kustepe Yolu, Mecidiyeköy
Tel.: (212) 275 35 90
If you are looking for good antique furniture or collector's pieces, this is the place to go. The shops have good-quality merchandize, but their prices are rising rapidly.

Mustafa Kayabek
Tünel Geçici 12, Tünel, BEYOĞLU
Tel.: (212) 244 45 78
Mustafabey's shop selling Turkish antiques is one of the oldest in the city. Mustafa knows his business and evaluates his merchandize honestly, selling it at reasonable prices.

Mustafa Orhan Kinaci
Bankacılar Sok 1, EMINÖNÜ
(near Yeni Camii)
Tel.: (212) 527 10 63
This family business, which is almost 50 years old, is very well known. You will marvel at the antiques, jewellery and fine Anatolian carpets and kilims.

Raffi Portakal
Mim Kemal Öke Caddesi 19, NIŞANTAŞI
Tel.: (212) 241 71 81
Raffi Portakal is one of the most important specialists in manuscripts, bronzes and glass. However, you will not be able to

buy anything here, for Raffibey is an auctioneer and what you might think is a shop is in fact an exhibition room.

Selden Emre
Teşvikiye Caddesi 99/1, TEŞVIKIYE
Tel.: (212) 517 67 85
This shop, with its gilt-framed paintings, antique china, cushions and rugs, is as elegant as an Ottoman reception room.

Sofa Art and Antiques
Nuruosmaniye Caddesi 42, CAĞALĞLU
Tel.: (212) 527 41 42
A profusion of engravings, maps and calligraphic inscriptions are cleverly arranged on shelves, hung on walls or displayed on antique desks. This fantastic array is completed by pottery, miniatures, textiles, old carpets, silverware and Turkish works of art, old and contemporary.

MARBLED PAPERS

Füsun Arikan
Workshop: Mühürdar Yaverbey Sokak, Inci Apt. 10/1, MODA, Tel.: (216) 338 28 34
Home: Bahiriye Caddesi, Ileri Sokak, Ileri Apt. 22/4, KADIKÖY
Tel.: (216) 338 28 34
Mrs Arikan, who had an exhibition recently at the French Institute, paints beautiful marbled paper that is worth framing. Visits by appointment only.

Köksal Çiftçi
Karikatürcüler Dernegi, Yerebatan Sarnıçı Çıkışı, SULTANAHMET
Tel.: (212) 513 60 61
You will be impressed by the talent of this young painter, who has modernized the techniques of marbled painting, adding birds and flowers to the otherwise abstract designs.

Mustafa Düzgünman
Mustafa Düzgünman, who was a master of traditional techniques, passed his knowledge on to a team of craftsmen who today make marbled paper for the small boutiques around the Yesil Ev Hotel.

Sultanahmet Crafts Centre
Near the Yesil Ev Hotel, SULTANAHMET
Tel.: (212) 517 67 85
This charming old courtyard

near the Yesil Ev Hotel contains several small workshops where shoppers can find reproductions of *objets d'art* and traditional craft products such as bound books, miniatures, dolls, jewellery, china, lace and marbled painting, etc.

PIPES

It is in Turkey that the mineral known as meerschaum is quarried and Turkey, not surprisingly, is the place for pipes ranging from the classic to the ornate in style. In the *bedesten* in the heart of the Covered Bazaar, there are two shops: **Yerlieseport** (tel.: (212) 526 26 19) and **Antique 83** (tel.: (212) 512 06 14). Other interesting shops are in the Arasta Çarşi market, including **Bilâl Dönmez** (tel.: (212) 516 41 42) in Sultanahmet.

CARPETS

Unearthing the most beautiful carpet at the best price is as difficult as buying a work of art. The following addresses represent a small selection of the thousands of carpet dealers throughout Istanbul. Begin by exploring the shops round the Covered Bazaar to get an idea of what is available, but if you want to get an overall impression of the carpet market, you should also visit Nişantaşi or Kadiköy, where you will find excellent shops.

Adnan & Hasan
Covered Bazaar
Tel.: (212) 527 98 87
(see p. 174)
This is the place to go for Anatolian kilims at reasonable prices. Adnan and Hasan have a good selection of other carpets as well.

Arasta Bazaar
Behind the Blue Mosque, SULTANAHMET
The shops in the arcades of this market square, which have replaced the Ottoman Sultans' stables, offer a choice of kilims, carpets, jewellery and other souvenirs.

Hazal Hali
Mecidiyeköy Köprüsü Sokak 27-29, ORTAKÖY
Tel.: (212) 261 72 33
Distinguished old and new carpets and kilims, tastefully displayed.

Muhlis Günbattı
Perdeçilar Caddesi 48, Covered Bazaar
Muhlisbey, the owner, has been trading in the Covered Bazaar for almost 40 years, and has developed an eye for the most beautiful Turkish carpets and kilims—antique and modern— as well as the finest rugs from Uzbekistan and other Asian towns. He also stocks cushions and bags with designs inspired by the patterns on kilims.

Oztarakçı
Mim Kemal Öke Caddesi 5, NIŞANTAŞI
Tel.: (212) 240 37 88
Owner Güneş Öztarakçı is a charming man who has accumulated a vast stock of modern and antique carpets, some of which are over a hundred years old. Even the more modern patterns, including those used for made-to-order carpets, are based on traditional designs. You will also find a number of silk Hereke carpets here.

Şengör Halı
Cumhuriyet Caddesi 47/2, TAKSIM
Tel.: (212) 250 73 03
You will be lost in admiration before the carpets and kilims in this fashionable shop. They are mostly less than a hundred years old and are of Turkish, Caucasian or Iranian make. This establishment, which has been trading since 1919, is held in high esteem by Turks, many of whom bring their foreign friends here.

Şişko Osman
Halıcılar Caddesi 49, Covered Bazaar, BEYAZIT
Tel.: (212) 526 17 08
(see pp. 172, 175, 178)
This shop in the Covered Bazaar will not disappoint. It is frequented by expatriates living in Turkey and the prices are commensurate with its clientele.

POTTERY

Gorbon
Ecza Sokak, Safterhan 6, LEVENT
Tel.: (212) 264 03 78
Halaskargazi Caddesi 345/1, ŞIŞLI, Tel.: (212) 246 89 75
Bagdat Caddesi 306/A, ERENKÖY
Tel.: (216) 358 69 65
(see pp. 180, 181)
Few visitors to Turkey get the opportunity to discover this contemporary pottery, which is generally known only to connoisseurs. The splendid Gorbon dishes, vases, plant pots, jugs and lamps are made of a thick, smooth, porcelain decorated in delightful colours. New patterns appear each year. The prices are very reasonable.

Kütahya and Iznik
Sümerbank, Istiklal Caddesi 302, BEYOĞLU
Tel.: (212) 252 08 05
Sümerbank, Ihlamur Caddesi 19, BEŞIKTAŞ
Tel.: (212) 260 35 97
If you want to buy pottery from Kütahya in Anatolia, the Sümerbank shops are both well worth visiting. There is, however, a less well-known address that is also highly recommended. The shop in question sells pottery at factory prices and is situated in the gardens of Yıldız Park in Beşiktaş. It also makes pottery to order. For information call the Yıldız Porselen Fabrikasi, near the Malta Köşk in Yıldız Park, Beşiktaş. Tel.: (212) 260 23 70. Iznik ceramics, celebrated for the fine patterns, are harder to find in the shops, so do not hesitate to ask any antique dealer where he his buys stocks. The shop in Yıldız Park usually has some available, however.

TOURISM

Iliada Tourism Inc.
Valikonaği Caddesi, Ciftciler Apt 12/1, NIŞANTAŞI
Many visitors to Istanbul—be they tourists or businessmen— in search of an efficient, trustworthy and high-class travel agents, call on the services of Meyzi Baran. Mr Baran, who speaks perfect English and French, is the expert manager of Iliada Tourism Inc. His clients include royal families and executives in multinational companies, who know that for Meyzi nothing is impossible.

SUGGESTED READING

Istanbul has been the subject of an enormous number of travel books, historical works, and paintings and engravings and the following does not attempt to be a comprehensive bibliography. Some of the books listed below may be out of print.

Freely, John, *Istanbul*, Blue Guide, Black/Norton, 1991.
Freely, John and Hilary Sumner Boyd, *Strolling through Istanbul*, Kegan Paul International, London, 1987.
Gülersoy, Çelik, *A Guide to Istanbul*, n.d.You will find this book easily in Istanbul. The author has also published a series of books on individual palaces and on the Ottoman decorative arts. These can be bought at the Touring and Automobile Club (Türkiye Turing Ve Otomobil Kurumu) near Haghia Sophia.
Gürsel, Nedim, *Istanbul*, Editions Autrement, Paris, 1989.
Kelly, Laurence (intro.), *Istanbul: A Travellers' Companion*, Constable, London, 1987.

ILLUSTRATED BOOKS

Akozan, Feridun, *The Sait Halim Pasa Yali*, Ankara, n.d.
Atasoy, Nurhan, Afif Bahnassi and Michael Rogers, *The Art of Islam*, Flammarion/UNESCO, Paris, 1990.
Ertuğ, Ahmet, *Topkapi, the Palace of Felicity*, Ed. Haardt, n.d.
Ertuğ, Ahmet, *Istanbul, City of Domes*, n.d.
Deleon, J., *A Taste of Old Istanbul*, Istanbul Library, n.d.
Ertuğ, Ahmet, *A 19th-Century Album of Ottoman Sultans' Portraits*, Inan and Sura Kiraç Collection, n.d.
Goodwin, Godfrey, *A History of Ottoman Architecture*, Thames and Hudson, London, 1971.
Gülersoy, Çelik, *Çiragan Palace*, Istanbul Library, n.d.
Gülersoy, Çelik, *Dolmabahçe Palace and its Environs*, Istanbul Library, 1990.
Gülersoy, Çelik, *The Caïque*, Istanbul Library, n.d..
Gülersoy, Çelik, *Taksim*, Istanbul Library, n.d.
Gülersoy, Çelik, *The Khedives and Çubuklu Summer Palace*, Türkiye Turing Ve Otomobil Kurumu, n.d.
Hellier, Chris, *Splendors of Istanbul: Houses and Palaces along the Bosporus*, Abbeville Press, New York, 1992.
Küçükerman, O., *Türk Evi, Turkish House*, Türkiye Turing Ve Otomobil Kurumu, n.d.

Lane, A., *Early Islamic Pottery; Later Islamic Pottery*, n.d.
Levey, Michael, *The World of Ottoman Art*, London, 1975.
Llewellyn, Briony, and Newton, Charles, *The People and Palaces of Constantinople: Watercolours by Amadeo Count Preziosi 1816-1882*, London, 1985.
Pick, Christopher (ed.), *Embassy to Constantinople; The Travels of Lady Mary Wortley Montagu*, Century, London, 1988.
Rogers, J. M. (ed.), *The Topkapi Saray Museum; Architecture: The harem and other buildings*, Thames and Hudson, London, 1986.

ESSAYS AND MEMOIRS

Atil, Esin (ed.), *Turkish Art*, Smithsonian Institution, Washington, D.C., 1980.
Barber, Noel, *The Sultans*, New York, 1973.
Berchet, Jean-Claude, *Le Voyage en Orient: Anthologie des Voyageurs Français dans le Levant au XIXe Siècle*, Editions Robert Laffont, Paris, 1985.
Burnaby, Captain Fred, *On Horseback Through Asia Minor*, A. Sutton, 1985.
Cuddon, J. A., *The Owl's Watchsong: A Study of Istanbul*, Century Classics, 1986.
Davis, Fanny, *The Ottoman Lady: A Social History, 1718-1918*, Greenwood Press, London, 1986.

Dwight, H. G., *Constantinople—Settings and Traits*, New York, 1907.
Eldem, Sedad Hakki, *Reminiscences of the Bosphorus*, Istanbul, 1979.
Esin, Emel, *A History of Pre-Islamic and Early Islamic Turkish Culture*, Istanbul, 1980.
Freely, John, *Stamboul Sketches*, n.d.
Garnett, Lucy M. J., *Turkish Life in Town and Country*, London, 1904.
Gautier, Théophile, *Constantinople: Istabul en 1982*, Isis, Paris, 1990.
Goytisolo, Juan, *Estambul Otomano*, Editorial Planeta, Barcelona, n.d.
Hindle, Tim, *The Sultan of Berkeley Square*, Macmillan, n.d.
Le Corbusier, *Journey to the East*, trans. I. Zaknic, MIT Press, Cambridge, Mass.,1989.
Loti, Pierre, *Constantinople fin de siècle*, Editions du Complexe, 1991.
Loti, Pierre, *Suprêmes Visions d'Orient: Fragments de Journal Intime*, Paris, 1921.
Mansel, Philip, *Sultans in Splendour: The Last Years of the Ottoman World*, Andre Deutsch, London, 1988.
Penzer, N. M., *The Harem*, London, 1936.
Rice, David Talbot, *Constantinople*, London, 1965.
Severin, Tim, *Jason Voyage: The Quest for the Golden Fleece*,

Arrow Books, London, 1986.
Shaw, Stanford J., and Eze Kural Shaw, *History of the Ottoman Empire and Modern Turkey*. Volume 2: *Reform Revolution, and Republic: The Rise of Modern Turkey, 1808-1975*, Cambridge University Press, New York, 1977.
Tuglaci, Pars, *The Role of the Balian Family in Ottoman Architecture*, Istanbul, 1990.

NOVELS

Gürsel, Nedim, *Le dernier tramway*, Editions du Seuil, Paris, 1991.
Loti, Pierre, *Aziyadé*, Kegan Paul International, London, 1989.
Mourad, Kenizé, *Farewell Princess*, Arrow Books, London, 1991.

REVIEWS AND MAGAZINES

Cornucopia.
An elegant magazine in English, which is published three times a year in Istanbul. It covers art, design and travel.

Istanbul, The Guide.
A monthly guide published in English and edited by Lale Apa. It has interesting articles covering all districts of the city as well as a diary section with all the best places to go.

ISTANBUL CALENDAR

FEBRUARY-MARCH-APRIL
Ramadan.
The date for the fast of Ramadan changes every year, taking place twelve days later on our calendar from the Ramadan of the previous year. It involves a month of fasting for Muslims, who are only allowed to eat or drink between sunset and sunrise. Ramadan provides the visitor with the chance to sample traditional nightly meals in certain restaurants, in Beykoz for example.

The Sugar Festival (Şeker Bayram), which lasts three days, marks the end of the Ramadan fast. It will take place in mid-April in 1995. People celebrate by giving each other sweets. The Covered Bazaar is closed.

MARCH-APRIL
International Film Festival.

APRIL
Tulip Festival in Emirgan.
During April the whole park

blooms with this flower, which originated in Turkey.
23 April: Festival of the Child.
Atatürk gave children power for one day of the year. A children's procession is held.

MAY-JUNE
The Sacrifice Festival (Kurban Bayram), or Sheep Festival, takes place ten weeks after Ramadan (it will be at the end of June in 1995). Most shops and businesses are closed for four days, including the Covered Bazaar.

JUNE-JULY
Festival of Art and Culture.
Concerts of classical music, jazz and performances of operas and ballets are put on in the some of the most spectacular locations in Istanbul. In the past, there have been performances of operas such as Mozart's *Die Entführung aus dem Serail* in Topkapı Palace, concerts in the wonderful little church of Saint Irene (so often closed when not in use for occasions such as this) and shows at the delightful little

theatre in the harem of Yıldız Palace.

OCTOBER
29 October: National holiday of the Turkish Republic.
Processions and parades through the city.

NOVEMBER
International Antiques and Decorative Arts Fair.
Remarkable auctions are held in the armoury at Yıldız Palace during this fair.

Page numbers in *italics* refer to illustrations.

ACKNOWLEDGEMENTS

Caroline Champenois and Jérôme Darblay would like to express their great appreciation to all the people who invited them into their homes and shared their lifestyles, with special thanks to the following:

Mr Hale Arpacioglu, Mr Bedri Baykam, Mr and Mrs Lale and Aloç Çavdar, Mr and Mrs Irem and Selçuk Erez, Mr Akan Ezer, Mr Zeynep Garan, Mr Mehmet Güleryüz, Mr Cemil Ipekçi, Mr Murat Morova, Mr Yaman Mursaloğlu, Mrs Ayşegül Nadir, Mr Daniel Ohotski, Mr Ali Réza Topçu, Mr and Mrs Ayşegül and Mr Tayfun Uzunova, Mr Ferhunde Verdi, Mr Fatoche Yalin as well as Mr Frédéric Delteil, Mr Eric Félicès and particularly Mrs Nicole Meyrat for their assistance with the photography.

The publishers would like to thank all the people in Istanbul who welcomed them with such great charm and warmth and who introduced the different aspects of the city, as well as all the Parisians who contributed to the success of this volume:

Mrs Suay Aksoy, Mr Çetin Anlagan, Lale Apa, Mr Abdükadir Ateş, the Turkish Minister of Tourism, Mrs Şennur Aydin, Mr Meyzi Baran, Mrs Oye Başak and Mr Affan Başak, Mr Yğit Bener, Mr and Mrs Benli, Mr Claude Bernard, Mr Tansug Bleda, the Turkish ambassador to France, Mrs Lale Bulak, Mr Jean-Michel Casa, of the French consulate in Istanbul, Mr Mordo Dinar, Mr François Dopffer, the French ambassador to Turkey, Mr Haldun Dormen, Mr Michael Dover, Mrs Demet Erginsoy, Mr Ahmet Ertuğ, Mr Nedim Esgin, Mr and Mrs Selçuk and Irem Erez, Mr John Freely, Mrs Sevgi Gonül, Mrs Sabine Greenberg, Mr Tony Greenwood, Mr Eric Grünberg, Mr Çelik Gülersoy, Mr Nedim Gürsel, Mr Korel Güyman, undersecretary to the Minister of Tourism, Mr Vitali Hakko, Mr and Mrs Hanci, Mrs Florence Hernandez, Mr Robert Hyda, Mrs Funda Keus, Mrs Suna Kiraç, Mr Rahmï Koç, Mrs Claire Lagarde, Mr Gérard-Georges Lemaire, Mr Yalcin Manav, Mrs Nevim Menemencioğlu, Mrs Kenizé Mourad, Mr Ayşegül Nadir, Mr François Neuville, Mrs Onat of Turkish Airlines, Mr Gultekin Ozkan, Mrs Yvonne Panitza, the management of the Pera Palas, Mr Richard Perle, Mrs Nicole and Mr Hugh Pope, Mr Fakir Sağlar, the Turkish Minister of Culture, Mr John Scott, Mrs Serena Sutcliffe, Mrs Azize Taylor, Mr Biltin Toker, Mr Artun Ünsal.

The publisher would also like to thank Turkish Airlines and its director, Mr Tezcan Yaramanci, for the tickets they graciously made available to the contributors to this book.

PICTURE CREDITS